THE JOURNAL NON/FICTION PRIZE

T0158284

Brief Interviews
with the
Romantic Past

Kathryn Nuernberger

MAD CREEK BOOKS, AN IMPRINT OF
THE OHIO STATE UNIVERSITY PRESS
COLUMBUS

Copyright © 2017 by The Ohio State University.
All rights reserved.
Mad Creek Books, an imprint of The Ohio State University Press.

Library of Congress Cataloging-in-Publication Data
Names: Nuernberger, Kathryn, author.
Title: Brief interviews with the romantic past / Kathryn Nuernberger.
Description: Columbus : Mad Creek Books, an imprint of The Ohio State University
    Press, [2017] | Includes bibliographical references. | Winner of the 2016 The
    Ohio State University Press/"The Journal" Non/Fiction Collection Prize
Identifiers: LCCN 2017006988 | ISBN 9780814254097 (pbk. ; alk. paper) | ISBN
    0814254098 (pbk. ; alk. paper)
Classification: LCC PS3614.U85 A6 2017 | DDC 814/.6—dc23
LC record available at https://lccn.loc.gov/2017006988

Cover design by Regina Starace
Text design by Juliet Williams
Type set in Sabon

♾ The paper used in this publication meets the minimum requirements of the
American National Standard for Information Sciences—Permanence of Paper for
Printed Library Materials. ANSI Z39.48–1992.

9 8 7 6 5 4 3 2 1

For my parents

CONTENTS

THE AIR LOOM

"If it be a Fact, a Veil should be drawn over it, as an Imperfection in human Nature."

FLOAT, CLEAVE

Like most everything, the history of hot air balloons is a history of sex and tragic death. In response to a suggestion that "the desire to float passively upon the currents of the air represent[s] the female principle while the urge to cleave through them upon aggressive wings typifies the male," L. T. C. Rolt, author of the seminal history *The Aeronauts,* insists, "The fact is that the floaters were the first to win the skies and it is with their victory that we are here concerned. It could not be claimed as a victory for feminism." His tone is one of revulsion at the very suggestion a man's gambit might take a woman's form. "To be borne aloft for the first time by a frail envelope of paper or silk a man needed as much courage as a tower jumper."

I try not to talk about being a woman because I don't want to be defined that way. I try not to talk about religion or politics because I am at odds with the people where I live. I try not to talk about my opinions, because who cares. I try not to talk at all, but sometimes I find myself saying just anything. Did you know, I once told the men at the coffee shop who wring their hands over socialized medicine, that there have been times being a woman was so different from being a man it was easier to imagine yourself a drifting balloon than the man below trying to steer?

A well-known poet read at our university, and one of her poems was a metaphor for the female orgasm as a bird beating its wings like a second heartbeat. I returned to my office to find one of the professors of the old guard waiting in the hallway to ask if this is, in fact, how the female orgasm feels. I had been a professor myself for less than two months at this point, so I changed the subject. He asked again, and I suggested he ask his wife. Not one to be put off, he said, "I'm not asking my wife. I'm asking you."

He's a jolly and affable man, and urgent curiosity about questions related to the pleasure of others is to be commended. Nevertheless, I told him to leave my office and take his sexual harassment with him. I didn't know what kind of person I was going to have to be then. I was wearing a new pair of dress slacks and never spoke of my still-nursing child who I sometimes could see in a fountain at the center of campus beside her father, who gave a little wave toward my window.

That night I was impatient for my daughter to go to bed so I could ask my husband, "Can't you feel it for yourselves? The bird pulsing to the nest?"

"I thought I was the bird."

Tomorrow I will eat in the school cafeteria with this professor and my now kindergarten-aged daughter, who says he is her best friend. He will ask her difficult questions, like, "What is it like to be young?" "Well," she'll say, chewing her French fry like a cigar she's been contemplating as the sun goes down, "sometimes it can be exasperating to be five, but mostly it's pretty good."

Then we'll talk over the child's head for a while about his wife's diagnosis, which he is right to worry about. Everyone in this little town we all share adores her for how she often appears at a convenient moment to pull her husband out of an intense conversation by his elbow. I've lived inside my careful silence so long, though, I prefer not to see him nudged away. When he told me about her prognosis, it was a secret. If she lived, there was still a lot the disease could take from her. Some things are harder to tell than that you are going to die, but some things are also hard to know alone. I write the history of aeronauts instead.

When Benjamin Franklin's gout got so bad it took four strong men to carry him into assembly, he made sketches for the patent office of a hydrogen-balloon-chair apparatus that would require only one man lightly steering. How can you not admire a person who thinks of air before wheels?

I wish I had told my friend that of course an orgasm is like a second heart beating a wing-flapping bird. That's why the poem was so good. Even I didn't know there was a bird in there, but now I feel it every time. I should have thanked him for asking.

"AND NOW BRIGHTNESS
FALLS FROM THE AIR . . ."

There is no question of ascending without the Bengal Lights, since slow burning baskets of blue glow hanging around the gondola are the only way the audience might see Sophie Blanchard's white dress and hat of ostrich plumes wind-whipped in the night sky as she stands free-ballooning in her basket the size of a child's cradle. Napoleon didn't name her the Chief Air Minister of Ballooning for nothing.

The reporters said she had an ugly face and nervous disposition. Nothing so startled her as a horse-drawn carriage. They said of this first lady of the air, proud of their cleverness, "A woman in a balloon is either out of her element or too high in it."

In daylight she carried up little dogs in parachutes to drop back down. In night, she had a boom ring of rockets and cascades around her basket. Who can look away from someone so flamboyant and vulnerable holding on to an invisible string?

She once climbed so high to avoid a hailstorm she lost consciousness and spent fourteen-and-a-half hours airborne.

She once put down in Turin with a nosebleed of icicles across her face.

If it is true and not English propaganda that Napoleon asked her to prepare for an aerial invasion by balloon, her assessment was the simple truth that it was not feasible.

On her first lift, her husband was standing next to her in the basket they shared, heavy and clumsy beneath the huge patchwork canvas of the old balloon that had made him Jean-Pierre Blanchard, Professor of Aeronautical Spectacle, the kind of man who could leave a wife and four children to balloon across the continent and then, when the dogs of bankruptcy would not float, take a Sophie out of the crowd and into the sky. She described it as "une sensation incomparable."

Or maybe she pursued him. In the only extant portrait of her, her visage is carefully shaded to fill out her nose and cheeks and the shadow cast by her fringe of bangs, while her neck, dress, and balloon are etched in simple lines, so that her head looks like an oval photocopy from another picture glued onto this one. The effect is not aesthetically pleasing, but it is confusing enough to keep you looking.

In his youth, Jean-Pierre ascended on horseback to make an impression. Another time he and Sophie crashed together. He suffered a serious head injury, and she was rendered mute for several weeks.

He was old and she was young when he had a heart attack in the basket. In some accounts it is said he fell from the air seizing at his chest and died a year later of injuries related to the fall.

To be in a balloon at night is to seem as if you are part not only of the wind but of the darkness. It is as if you yourself were without substance or shape.

Once he was gone, Sophie could ascend in a much smaller balloon, using significantly less hydrogen. The fireworks were her idea. Never rich, she paid off his creditors and had savings enough to spare.

She offered to ascend as a benefit for a home for fallen women, her profession having much in common with the work of prostitutes, but the director declined, because she could not bear to see another woman risk her life.

The full-color print of her crash from the roofs of Paris as her balloon sets the block on fire is stunning. This is because the deep orange of the flames is perfectly offset by the deep blue of the night. Her white dress of a body cleaves the foreground of flames. "Beautiful! Beautiful! Vive Madame Blanchard!" someone shouted, not realizing what was happening. And then later: "It lighted up Paris like an immense moving beacon."

THE GAZELLE

Benjamin Franklin, always thinking, wondered, "Who can afford so to cover his Country with Troops for its defenses, as that Ten Thousand Men descending from the clouds might not in many places do an infinite deal of mischief before a Force could be brought together to repel them?"

It took longer than you might expect for the history of balloons to intersect with the history of warfare.

In 1870 it was a balloon that broke the Siege of Paris. The pilot left with baskets of carrier pigeons to send back in with microfilmed intelligence tied to their feet.

A decade earlier and a war apart, it was dangerous to put a balloon down south of the Mason-Dixon line. They'd hang you sure as shit for Yankee bedevilment and espionage.

Union balloons infuriated and frightened the Confederates. To them it was a sort of panopticon hanging there in the sky, and they wasted many bullets firing at it. Seeing it made them feel as if it were seeing you.

A balloon required too many resources to be practical, but the Confederate men loved to spy their own, *The Gazelle,* hovering in the distance. It was stitched together out of ball gowns they thought they remembered, though many of the soldiers were so poor and barefoot from dirt farms it was the dream of a ball gown they fought for.

Those boys had a way of putting their eyes on a distant fixed point and never letting them wander. You can call that courage, but it's a lot of other things too. There were people all around in the field, dressing wounds or starving or humming an old song like there's nothing else in this life. But the Southern soldier, as the story goes, only ever had eyes for the square patch of green silk that was his girl floating above the river line.

THE BLUE SKY,
THE GRAY WOODS

Whether Elisabeth Thible was ever satisfied is not something we can say. Aside from reports from the day she was the first woman to go up in a balloon, her name is invisible in the archives.

Jean-Baptiste de Laurencin gave her his seat in the basket because in January he'd been in *Le Flesselle,* which crash-landed after twelve minutes in the air, and it was enough for him to fall once. The other men let her have his seat because of how everyone who went up talked about the strange and unexpected beauty of sound up there. *In that unearthly stillness familiar sounds from far below, the bark of a dog, a voice calling, even a torrent of wind rushing through trees, though uncannily clear, had a poignantly remote quality.* Elisabeth Thible was an opera singer, and she went up dressed as Minerva singing from Monsigny's *La Belle Arsène.*

Arsène is a woman who could never be made happy. When asked by a fairy what might relieve her sorrow, she said she wanted to be carried into the fairy's beautiful sphere. You can imagine how long she was content with a castle in the clouds. By the second day, the fountains had lost their sparkle and plash. By the third, she was thrown out of the air into the gray woods, where she found herself on the run from a growling din of bears. She fell into the grip of a woodcutter who offered her shelter, but only if she would cook for him and do other things as well. The stage directions indicate she exits left flung over his shoulder and kicking. Because it was the eighteenth century, it turned out rape and a kettle pot suited her and brought her satisfaction at last. Monsigny's reputation is as the first comic librettist.

There are no accounts of how Elisabeth's voice carried or whether it is unearthly to hear the notes go up as the notes went up. The lyrics "I want to go to the divine sphere, make for me your beautiful paradise, where I do not have to carry anyone else along" were swept by the breeze over the onlookers' open mouths.

She was so quickly forgotten that a few years later, when André-Jacques Garnerin wanted Citoyenne Henry to go up in a basket with him, the officials thought a woman in the air had never been done before. Garnerin pleaded his case before a tribunal in Paris that wanted to know how the reduced air pressure would affect a female's delicate organs. And then he had to appeal the ruling.

The next tribunal relented to let her go, and the public could call such a woman what they would. Garnerin made a fine spectacle of it by cutting loose the balloon and opening the first parachute for an astonishing and magnificent descent. After that we never hear of her again either, so it is impossible to say whether she was any more satisfied than Elisabeth to be done with air.

La Belle Arsène is based on Voltaire's poem "La Béguele," which is the origin of the famous line, "The perfect is the enemy of the good," though there is a great deal of debate about the accuracy of that translation.

A Thin Blue Line

The summer was the greenest since we moved to this farm at the edge of a town where I practice keeping quiet and other forms of politeness. In the evenings I would pull stinging nettles from around the young pumpkins with Rachel, who was the first person here I spoke to freely. Even though she is practically a witch in her own right for what she knows about plants and tinctures—she could brew an abortion for you out of what's growing in my pasture if the pending legislation in these parts goes as badly as it might—she had never heard the old story about the sister who gathered such nettles and stomped them into flax to sew into shirts to throw around the necks of her cursed swan brothers to save them back to princes.

It was also the summer when Rachel's son, Theo, couldn't get out of bed most days and didn't eat and reminded us all that it's pretending to think he'll live forever. But we didn't talk about it much, because how can you?

There was an evening when he was feeling good, so he came out to pick cucumbers for his brothers, who eat them like apples, and I gave him a side hug and said, "I'm happy to see you," and he said in that wry way of teenagers who are happy but keeping it cool—"Yeah. The boy lives."

It was the summer I talked instead about phlogiston, which was an early explanation for why sparks float up and why we exhale something lighter than what we inhale. When a gas one-third of the weight of air was discovered in 1766, every scientist on and off the continent spent the summer filling calf bladders to bounce around their laboratories. Phlogiston, they thought, was why the aeronauts could one day send their balloons right up to the edge of the atmosphere to discover that in fact there is an atmosphere.

Watching the Montgolfier brothers' huge balloon drift off, an old woman began to cry. Coming right to the edge of understanding does that to me sometimes too, but the way she explained it was, "Alas! When they have discovered the means of escaping death, I shall not be able to take advantage of it."

When Theo is feeling good he does magic tricks for us. He likes to pull numbers out of the air, and he can make an egg bounce. He keeps a little collection of riddles, which are and are not magic tricks. He has a theory that he's died before and he will again and that it's like leveling up in a video game. He never makes his brothers give him a turn with the controller, so we just sit on the couch together and watch the pixilated prince zip and jump in a blur of green across the black screen of sky.

The sister was sewing against the clock. She couldn't speak, she only had seven years, her husband the king saw her picking nettles in the graveyard and thought she was a witch. Rachel and I laughed at this part, because what can you do but laugh to realize it is his flames licking at her ankles as she flings the shirts into the air to catch around the necks of a descending flock of belligerent and wing-beating swans?

In the end all is made right. The newly unenchanted princes save her from the fire, the king promises never to burn his beloved wife at the stake again. The youngest brother, alas, was a sleeve short, and had to live with a single wing dangling off his body like a form of amputation or miracle. Against all odds, he grew very old that way and loved to charm children by making it seem he had plucked a feather from behind one of their ears like magic.

There were of course days when he tried to button a shirt and he couldn't help but curse that wing, but later, when all of his brothers were gone and also his sister, he'd look down at it tenderly, that treasured gift from the summer he came back down from the air.

HEED NOT
THE MILK HARE

The princess of Hesse-Rhinevelt was among the most beautiful and eligible on the list of ninety-nine who might become queen but was cut in the first round because her mother had been in the habit of giving birth alternately to daughters and hares.

This was not a problem without precedent. In 1726 in England Mary Toft was startled into miscarriage by the sight of a rabbit. Later that day she "delivered of a creature resembling a Rabbet but whose Heart and Lungs grew without its Belly." About fourteen days hence she was delivered of "a perfect rabbet." "From that Time," it was said, "she hath not been able to avoid thinking of Rabbets." A few days after came four more, until there were nine, all of whom died "bringing into the World."

For all this she was attended by her mother-in-law, who was also a midwife, but John Howard, a man-midwife of thirty years experience was called to account. He delivered from Mary's body "three legs of a Cat of a Tabby colour, and one leg of a Rabbet: the guts were as a Cat's and in them were three pieces of the Back-Bone of an Eel." It was supposed the cat's feet were formed in her imagination from a cat Mary was fond of who slept on her bed at night.

I think we need to pause here and discuss miscarriage. If you know a woman who has had a baby, you probably know a woman who has had a miscarriage. If you have not had a miscarriage, you likely do not know that dilation and curettage is a standard procedure now, performed under anesthesia to remove the material of the pregnancy so that you do not bleed and bleed for weeks and do not develop an infection in the uterus as material of the pregnancy begins to decay.

Doctors have a great many words that are meant to sound almost but not quite like the experience you are having. I think of this as a specialized form of politeness. I try to be polite in return, so I did not say anything about the strange and hurtful words "missed abortion" on my paperwork as I left the emergency room. I did not say, "I am too sad to let you cut and suck 'the material' of my pregnancy out of my body." I did not ask if the baby would still have a body after it was done. I did not explain that I had been shown horrific animations of abortion in Catholic school sex ed that were very much on my mind right now, but also that I could still tell the difference between my life and another woman's. Since it was not a symptom of anything, I didn't mention I was having trouble separating the idea of tissue they wanted to clean out of me from the ultrasound picture I still carried in my wallet. I just went home and bled and bled and suffered a great many oddly shaped things to pass from my body that were clots and pieces of placenta and a little mew of a 13-week fetus.

By 1727 John Howard was offering to deliver these rabbits from Mary before anyone who asked. According to one account, "The last leap'd twenty three Hours in the Uterus before it dy'd." Elsewhere it was written, "As soon as the eleventh Rabbet was taken away, up leap'd the twelfth."

By the time the British Royal Family had grown interested in the case, Mary Toft was strangely squeezing her legs together, complaining of a severe pain in her right side, and Howard would not let anyone assist in the deliveries. The royal surgeon, Sir St. André, delivered of her what he thought was a hog's bladder. He was fully convinced and quick to publish an account, as it proved his theory of sympathetic medicine. Keeping pets in your house, he cautioned, would give your child a dogface, or harelip, or otherwise allow the mind to inflict its impressions on the body. He wrote of Mary herself that she possessed a healthy and strong constitution, a fair complexion and was "of a very stupid and sullen temper: she can neither write nor read."

In general doctors dislike their patients. I understand why and try to be polite and use the words they prefer to be used and be as nonplussed about my condition as they are, but nevertheless I can feel in the room our distaste for each other. After six weeks passed we were all beside the ultrasound machine once again, looking at some material we had started to call the circus peanut. I wouldn't ever stop bleeding until it was gone it seemed, so the surgery was scheduled for the next morning. I lay in the bed that night telling my body all through my body, "It's okay to let go now, it's okay to let go now." And in the morning there was the peanut, not wavy and gray on a screen, but gelatinous and rounded on this side of the world. When I arrived at the hospital explaining it was done on its own after all, I had never seen a person so irritated with me as that doctor was.

Members of the Court deliberated at length over this strange case. One position was, "If it be a Fact, a Veil should be drawn over it, as an Imperfection in human Nature." Others, who wished to know all things, sent the scientist and doctor, Samuel Molyneaux, to investigate further. He found on the rabbits drawn from her body evidence of cutting with a man-made instrument, as well as pieces of straw and grain in their droppings. Then Mary Toft's husband was caught buying live rabbits at the market. I'll admit, I was a little surprised to discover it was really just a hoax. I thought she'd also reached the limits of language.

Faced with so much evidence, Mary confessed an old woman passing through the edge of her town had promised her a way to ensure she'd never want for anything again. After the miscarriage of a baby who did not look like a baby but did look like some sort of soft creature a mother could love, her cervix was still open and malleable. And so she took heed and began to insert various animal parts into her body to be born anew.

She went to prison for a year at Tothill Fields Bridewell, and when she emerged in 1727, she had given birth to a human daughter. While she was away Dr. Molyneaux died of poisoning and Dr. St. Andre eloped with his widow. Everyone believed St. Andre poisoned Molyneaux, but no one could prove it, so he lived happily ever after.

It was suggested Mary Toft's old woman might well have been a milk hare. A milk hare is a witch who takes on a rabbit's form to steal milk from the neighbors' cows in the night. The only way to catch such a one as her is to shoot or otherwise wound the witch-in-hare. You will know her later by how you find the selfsame wound on her woman body as you put on that dash of a wretched rabbit you never could catch.

Introduction to the Symbols of the Revolution

My husband is not interested in reading about Marie Antoinette's hair. "Isn't this a little girly for you?" he says.

I show this man everything I write because he gives the best advice of anyone I know. He gives it in a way that is harsh, even when complimentary, which I appreciate because it's the only way I can trust that it's true, because I'm one of these people who feels every character is a metaphor for something wrong with me. I never saw a witch burn that I didn't imagine was one of you burning me. I'm also like those villains who don't realize they might be on the outside of the pyre looking in.

A great many of the women I admired as a child were lit on fire. Based on the books in my library, it seemed being chained naked to a stake and martyred by the Romans for threatening the emperor's faith and power was the closest a girl could get to being smart about something.

My husband is not intrigued by the incongruity of writing about power and gender via metaphors of hair. He also does not like to be called sexist and doesn't appreciate being lumped in with all the other sexists we know. He doesn't like it when I talk about tone-policing, micro-aggression, or victim-blaming in regard to something as superficial as a despot's giant, preposterous wig, about which he is tired of reading.

Was the tallest style called the hedgehog? So what?

Was it so high they had to raise the doors to the cathedral like it was some kind of massive middle finger wobbling atop the heads of these ladies? Who cares?

Did the young queen try to make political statements by sticking a model warship of the *Belle Poule* frigate on top of the thing? Tragic, but boring.

Did some rich white woman tuck miniature figurines of a black slave breastfeeding the young duke into her pouffe alongside a replica of a beloved parrot eating cherries? Of course she did.

I tell him he's proving my point. He tells me I'm proving his.

Everyone was looking at Marie Antoinette looking at everyone looking at herself. It's like when I go to the office and he stays home with the kid and he sees no one all day and I try to keep my chin up as I stop and chat with colleague after colleague in our little cinderblock hall of mirrors of a general classroom building. He wants to know if I'd like to trade places. I would, but that *Belle Poule* frigate has sailed.

In the corridors of windowless geometry I pretend I never think about my hair or worry if it's the hair of a frumpy woman no one wants to hear speak, and also I try not to touch it while we're talking business around the conference table. Those meetings must never include mention of how I only pretend not to think about my hair or worry how it's affecting the way I am perceived, because around the conference table we've all agreed to pretend everything about us is exactly the same and anyway a man never wonders what I'm thinking about his hair and it's been agreed I should try to be more like him.

When I pass the other women from this conference table in the hall, we often pause to compliment each other's dresses or shoes or hair, because it is a quick and easy way we know how to be pleasant, and though it is boring, it is a relief to be successfully pleasant to someone you are passing in the hallway on the way to going where you wish to be. Like when Marie Antoinette ascended the scaffold, she stepped on the executioner's toe and then she said, "Pardon me, sir, I did not mean to do it." To which he replied, "No Madam, pardon me."

Dear husband, I know a charm we can try that will help you help me brush out this tangle. If you will be my hairdresser, I will be yours and we will make a little circle of braiding like the girls do on the playground, each one saying something she heard about the one in front in a game of gossip telephone until all the metaphors are nothing but notions you can pin for decoration. You can cover your hair in butterflies, swarms of cupids, or marching squadrons. A melancholy person could choose a single crematory urn. Another sort could put a bird in a cage in there to sing from its little swinging perch. Whatever you want to be, now you can be that, within the confines of your hair.

Or, if you prefer, I will be like the princess was when she first arrived at court—the portrait shows her astride a horse, wearing pants, rearing up in emulation of the Sun King. I will not say I am worried about how such a symbol might be received. I will not mention the letters from my mother in Austria, chastising me to keep my figure and conceive an heir. We will never speak a word of my husband the prince, who for seven years has been unable to ejaculate into my body.

I will not foresee that after waiting so long for a child I could lose the love of the people by giving birth to a daughter and then baptizing her with all the pomp and expense they would have seen given a son. The Duc d'Orleans has been hording grain to foment the revolution, but I will not worry my pretty little head over this. Because it was forbidden by the king, I will not have read Diderot's *Encylopedia,* including George Danton's entry about wigs and why we need them—"All borders are dangerous. If left unguarded, our categories could collapse, and our world dissolve into chaos." When the mob storms the palace, they will have loaves of bread on pikes. When the mob returns to Paris, they will have the heads of men on pikes and they will stop at the wigmaker's on the way to have those heads powdered with flour.

We will step back a few feet in the gallery, my husband and I, holding hands and admiring the stallion's wild eyes, my fearless bold gambit of a modest bun tucked beneath a jaunty and masculine costume, how it's going to change everything. He will say, "Now that. That is interesting."

ON HORSEBACK

As an exercise in empathy and imagination, I like to walk through portrait galleries and try to know each oil painting. I do this alone. In the Brun de Versoix of 1783, Marie Antoinette is riding in trousers.

If I were the kind of person who could stand going to the outlet mall with the ladies, I might appreciate the fashion statement in and of itself and I wouldn't be rambling in the car to bored yawns about the political gambit at stake here. The stallion is drawn up into a bold rearing stance, in imitation of the heroic and mythologizing depictions of the Sun King. Would his grandson, Louis XV, notice the homage? Would he notice it just barely and be charmed or would he really notice and be outraged?

Young Marie Antoinette loved to ride because the court could not keep up with her and because what else did she have to do with her day after day? She rode astride because she was under the impression a queen could do as she wished.

Her mother, the empress of Austria, begged her to give it up. She sent a letter every week: "Riding spoils the complexion, and in the end your waistline will suffer from it. Furthermore, if you are riding like a man, dressed like a man, as I suspect you are, I have to tell you that I find it dangerous as well as bad for bearing children—and that is what you have been called upon to do; that will be the measure of your success."

The letters do not address the problem that the dauphin would not deflower the dauphine because something was mysteriously amiss with his penis or his mind. Nor does the letter address the war Austria fought against France when the Empress Marie-Teresa, a woman, ascended the throne. She hardly speaks of the dozen cobbled-together marriages she arranged to make grandchildren of her enemies.

The Versoix is one of a great many portraits of Marie Antoinette. There is Marie with a book and Marie beneath a tower of her own hair. Marie with her children, Marie in a peasant dress. Marie as a cartoon of a fornicating ostrich, Marie riding a dildo over Paris, Marie looking haggard in the white shift that was the last dress she ever wore.

Fewer likenesses of Théroigne de Méricourt can be found, though even now for £14.58 you can buy a print of Ambrose Tardieu's pencil sketch from *Des Maladies Mentales*. There were a great many portraits of women made across the decades at Saltpêtrière, the asylum for women where mental maladies were considered scientifically; the collection only begins with Tardieu's sketches. I've studied most closely the photographs from a century later, which they took of hysterics, trying to understand the physiognomy of lunacy. Not me, them. I am trying to understand indifference and cruelty.

When I pull the book of these photographs out of my bag to ask if it seems like the women might be pretending these faces to give the doctors what they want, it is clear I do not understand the purpose of a ladies day out. I've been alone in a house with a baby day after day for several months now, so I don't know how else I could determine whether the faces of hysterical madness are really madness or just compliance, but I learn once more that I am too eager with my questions.

Théroigne de Méricourt is better known as the beautiful Amazon who led a band of starving women to the assault on Versailles. She went on horseback, astride, dressed as a man, to demand an audience of the king. She was so eager people whispered she was practically St. Joan, hysterical voices and all.

Before, she had been Anne-Josèph Théroigne, a child who was hungry, then later, a housemaid who was bored. She added de Méricourt as an artifice when she followed a nobleman to England and began her serious studies of etiquette and coquetry and taste. When everyone was whispering about the dauphine's refusal to wear the corset royal, Anne-Josèph knew enough to spit in the dirt of a queen who didn't want to be queen.

After securing her financial future and her father's and her brother's through arrangements with former lovers, she went to Italy to perform opera, but when the revolution came, "her insolent and rebellious character responded to and incarnated the revolt and protest of the masses. The frivolous courtesan was gone never to return." Which is to say, she made her way to the front of the crowd.

She said when she broke into the apartments of "that Austrian woman," Princess Lamballe looked like a lampshade running in those skirts, while Marie Antoinette shed powder from her falling-down hair as she fled.

As the revolution went on it became hard to choose the right side. Théroigne went with the Brisotins against the Jacobins. The Brisotins were moderate on the subject of executions and anarchy. Of course my sentiments lean toward the Brisotins too, but isn't it naïve to think there could be half-measures when the wealth and power of the landed gentry was at stake? We're eating soup and salads at the Olive Garden, shopping bags in a little pile around the legs of our chairs. No one can understand why I'm still going on about this.

Once Anne had helped a mob trample a nobleman and he died under her feet. She called the women of the revolution from their homes to organize and march, to form battalions, to fight as the men fight. The women came, which caused problems with the men who wanted equality and liberty but also meant brotherhood when they said brotherhood. Anne, the traitorous Brisotin woman, was only a temporary problem, though, because it was women who soon stripped her in the square and women who flogged her. When she died, it was in the Saltpêtrière, where women surrounded her and it is said their cacophony of wild screams is more than anyone could bear.

PLUTARCH'S
PARALLEL LIVES OF
VIRTUE AND FAILING

When Charlotte Corday left for Paris after the September massacres, she was carrying a copy of Plutarch's *Lives* and a kitchen knife with a six-inch blade.

Plagued by a chronic and debilitating skin condition that is never depicted in portraits, Jean-Paul Marat was known for conducting much of his business from his bath. There were rumors he bathed in the blood of his enemies. Jacques-Louis David's 1793 painting *The Death of Marat* shows only his own reddening the tub. The picture is described as the first modernist painting for how it "took the stuff of politics as its material and did not transmute it." To be sure, this is a painting with some journalistic integrity, although the artist moved the knife from Marat's chest, where Charlotte Corday left it, to the floor. And he removed Charlotte Corday, who waited in a corner to be arrested, from the scene entirely. In Marat's hand rests the note he had been reading, "Citizen, my extreme misery gives me a right to your benevolence."

So ended the summer of 1793, when, fearful of what would happen if the invading armies of neighboring monarchs freed the prisoners of France, who would no doubt turn on the people in a murderous rage, Marat of the Mountain, as he was known, called on the draftees to kill the prisoners before they marched to the front lines. By September half the prison population of Paris was dead.

At her trial, Charlotte Corday said, "I killed 1 man to save 100,000." Everyone in the room understood she was echoing Robbespierre, who said, "With regret I pronounce the fatal truth: Louis must die so that the nation may live," and who would soon replace Marat at the head of the Terror.

Harper's Weekly, covering the assassination of Abraham Lincoln in 1865, observed that Corday is the only assassin history has forgiven. And even she was a fool and a tool of her enemies. "The heart recoils, whatever the excuse, the instinct of mankind curses the assassin." In the famous painting, Marat's arm is draped over the lip of the tub like a mother whispering *pieta*. No one in the room of David's portrait suffers except Marat.

When the executioner brought the red shirt and scissors, she cut her own hair and handed a lock to the court room artist who had been completing her portrait, begun at the trial only hours before.

There was much debate after her death about the color of her hair. Her passport says chestnut, but people wanted to believe it had been lightened by powder. In the portrait it is brown and covered with a bonnet.

After her decapitation, a carpenter who made repairs to the guillotine lifted her head from the basket and slapped her on the cheek. Witnesses reported an expression of "unequivocal indignation" came over her face. This man was imprisoned for three months for his actions by order of the Jacobin councils, which also called for her body to be autopsied for the purpose of determining whether Charlotte Corday had been a virgin.

Reports indicate she was intact, which is one more fact that tells us nothing about whether she was virtuous or whether she failed.

Pantoum for Tilly Matthews

You make the lines, but you must also obey their rules of repeating. He called it the Air Loom. Run by Jack the Schoolmaster, his was a sewing machine fueled by putrid fumes. Expectorants from the anus of a horse. The Glove Woman works the shuttle.

He called it the Air Loom. Run by Jack the Schoolmaster. What else could explain 16,594 beheadings between September 1793 and July 1794? Expectorant from the anus of a horse. The Glove Woman works the shuttle. The machine assails us with brain sayings and dream workings.

What else could explain 16,594 beheadings between September 1793 and July 1794? A mad doctor must be cautious not to debate with lunatics. The machine assails us with brain sayings and dream workings. A doctor must be afraid to enter a perplexity of metaphysical mazes.

A mad doctor must be cautious not to debate with lunatics. Tilly's wife found him as lucid and gentle as he'd ever been. A doctor must be afraid to enter a perplexity of metaphysical mazes. For such good reason, she was barred from making further visits.

Tilly's wife found him as lucid and gentle as he'd ever been. The loom performs its apoplexies with a nutmeg grater. For such good reason, she was barred from making further visits. It weaves the fabric of aether into a warp of magnetic fluid.

The loom performs its apoplexies with a nutmeg grater. During the Terror he had been a brave and worthy English spy. It weaves the fabric of aether into a warp of magnetic fluid. He delivered support to the moderate Girondins pleading temperance.

During the Terror he had been a brave and worthy English spy. Mysterious gases must have brainwashed the politicians and the populace—he delivered support to the moderate Girondins pleading temperance. Such a machine could only be the work of undercover Jacobin terrorists and Bill the King.

Mysterious gases must have brainwashed the politicians and the populace. Awaiting the guillotine on charges of espionage. Such a machine could only be the work of Jacobin terrorists and Bill the King. He passed many years in that place.

Awaiting the guillotine on charges of espionage, he turned his faculties to uncovering the machine of human suffering. He passed many years in that place, devoted himself to making schematics of the thing with an engineer's mind and a draftsman's pen.

He turned his faculties to uncovering the machine of human suffering. You make the lines, but you must also obey the rules of their repeating. Devoted himself to making schematics of the thing with an engineer's mind and a draftsman's pen. His was a sewing machine fueled by putrid fumes.

Hearts in Jars

When I was back in my hometown for Thanksgiving, sitting on a leather couch in the white part of the neighborhood that raised me as best it could and sometimes not the best, watching the grand jury's ruling come down, I wondered if there were a right number of buildings to burn that would set the world right.

I mean, the revolutionaries burned down Paris and a great many things changed.

There were op-eds and uncles who talk like op-eds making up what they didn't know about black-owned businesses and city council elections and the incitements of outsiders. The turkey and drinking and consternation of my grandmother who kept pleading for us to stop talking politics started to feel like agreement with whoever got loudest, though I couldn't even always see what the loudest point was, since nobody comes right out and says they want to see a kid dead. They just don't want to see other people dead more.

I was very deep in my reading about Marie Antoinette then, so I tried on occasion to change the subject by asking questions like, "Did you know the last prince of France's heart is in a jar?" No one knew or cared, but you can't really stop me when I get going. Following a tradition of preserving royal hearts, it was smuggled out of the prison by Pelletin, the examining physician, who said he was startled by the scars covering the nine-year-old boy's body, as well as the size of the infected boils on his neck.

The heart was later stolen by the doctor's student, then given to an archbishop who held it until 1830, when it was sent to Spain, then on to a castle in Vienna. Now it rests in the cathedral at Saint Dennis, where they preserve the hearts of all the kings.

The history of white people is a history of cognitive dissonance, which is an even-tempered description of a distempered experience.

Watching the attorney general reading in the middle of a Friday night a cop's sworn testimony that a dead teenager had run toward the bullets like some sort of unstoppable beast—he paused, the white lawyer in the brown suit, to take a drink from a water bottle, and I thought even-tempered insanity must be the most dangerously violent variety.

When Haiti was Saint-Domingue, Julien Raimond was a free man of color who owned 100 people and an indigo plantation. Under Louis XIV he would have been considered white because the Sun King believed French blood to be so potent one drop was enough to turn a person French. Under Louis XVI it was otherwise.

Raimond moved to Paris in 1785 to argue the case for equal rights for free men of color before the French Colonial Ministry. The publication of the Declaration of the Rights of Man in 1789 gave him renewed hope that the Code Noir might be revised. Among other things, he wanted to be allowed to spell his family name, Raymond, as his father had.

When refused representation in the newly formed National Assembly, he published pamphlets objecting to taxation without representation. "We are proprietors, taxpayers, and, moreover, very useful," he wrote sensibly and pragmatically. But later he exhorted, with a less even temper, "We will not stop repeating that we are free, physically, morally, and politically, that we have regained possession of the inalienable rights of man."

Then he regains his composure and dismisses arguments for immediate abolition for reasons that involved a balance of rhetorical sophistication and self-preservation historians are not sure how to parse. "One could hardly suppose that I should want to ruin at one stroke my entire family, which possesses . . . seven or eight millions in property," he wrote.

Julien Raimond's mother was very wealthy, and this was at least part of what caught the attention of his white French father. Her fortune of a dowry was three times his.

When you look at Julien's portrait, you can easily imagine how white people who had good intentions would have told him through smiles that

he looked utterly white to them. Our minds so easily become the jars that
hold things other people have said.

Even if you've been reading about the French Revolution for eight
hours a day for eight months or more, it's still easy to forget all of the
white people were not white people. This is probably more or most or
only true if you yourself are white people who spent your childhood in
the company of white people saying things like, "Hypothetically, if you
were to date a black guy I would have no problem with that, but I would
wonder what you were trying to prove."

It was the duchess with the figurine of an African nurse in her hair
that reminded me to ask about the colonies and how they financed, or in
times of drought and revolt failed to finance, the monarchy.

Though there is no shortage of data on what a duchess might have
spent on tassels and pearl buttons and the bouquets she set into her hair
or the hair she bought from a peasant to braid into her own, I cannot find
any firm numbers on what Haiti contributed to the monarchy's attempts
to quash the revolution or the National Assembly's attempts to organize
itself after.

Here is what has been recorded: Haiti produced 40 percent of all the
sugar in Europe and the colonies, 60 percent of all coffee in Europe, one
million pounds of indigo, two million pounds of cotton.

Or what about my own city? Who pays the white boys from some out-
skirt of the metropolis to drive in each morning and buckle guns around
their waists? According to *The Atlantic*, Ferguson, Missouri, harvested
$2,635,400 in municipal court fines, which accounted for 20 percent of
the city budget. Eighty-five percent of traffic stops there involved black
motorists, even though the city is only 67 percent black, and its roads are
traveled every day by a large number of white commuters.

Jacques Necker, financial advisor to the king, said, in a rare moment
of honesty, "It is only by selling abroad the merchandise that it had gotten
from its colonies . . . that France obtains a positive balance."

Sometimes I drive around the streets of my childhood trying to figure
out how one part makes the other parts, and it's clear no one made the
machine. The machine made itself out of the patterns of happenings and
once the machine has its pattern, it fabricates. And it fabricates and fabricates, until it jams itself rusty or flints a spark.

I watched the news and wondered with which powdered wig of a
duchess I share the most in common.

As many as 100 false dauphins appeared over the years. So many
people wanted to believe there was still a prince.

On TV a man got dropped off in front of the courthouse. It was like when my husband drops me off at work in the morning and I cross the street waving goodbye. An ordinary moment made strange by how it was on the live feed streaming from the helicopter overhead. As he disappeared into the growing crowd, I thought how middle-aged and even-tempered the man looked in his polo and khaki pants, wearing his cell phone in a little case attached to his belt like nerdy men of my father's generation so often do. He was someone's uncle, or a father perhaps, afraid for what would become of his son someday.

Only in the last decade have genetic tests confirmed the heart in the jar really was the heart of the last dauphin. That little boy really died in prison in that terrible way. I wiped a tear from my eye to read that it was true. But what was I hoping for? That it would have turned out to be some other child's heart instead?

TRINKETS

The Hall of Mirrors in the Palace at Versailles is the most frightening room in all of Western civilization. In this room some of the cabinets are doors. Some of the mirrors are windows. In a time when mirrors were the most expensive thing a king could possess, 17 arches tiled with 21 mirrors each lined a narrow corridor gilded by as many courtiers begging an audience with the passing king. Some of the kings were enamored by costumes, spying, and punishment. All of their names were Louis. The painted ceiling shows Louis winning one battle and Louis winning another.

The dauphiné lands were purchased in 1349; henceforth the eldest son of the king was called dauphin, which also means dolphin. There are no dolphins in the Rhone or the Seine or the Rhine. The kings of Britain and Spain owned the seas. Nevertheless, the candelabra are dolphins, as are the mantle clocks. The drawer pulls on the swivel desk are interlaced with dolphins, so too the ewers, the inkwells, the door handles, the towel bars, the crest, the flag, the fountains (of course the fountains), the frames, the tasterin, the table legs, the dinner knives, forks, and spoons, the teapots, even the chenets that hold the fire logs.

His name means dolphin. His name means sun. His name means two cockerels fighting. His name means lily of the valley. His name means crystal. His name means silver. His name means brass. His name means king who will be king.

Louis XV had a mistress who would buy him little dolphin knick-knacks to show she'd been thinking of her king and the boy he'd once been. The mark of excellence in her position was that he should never once contemplate the precise nature of her thoughts or why she had them. Have you ever tried to erase yourself? I think about her choice to assume the position of official royal consort as being very much like a nun's in terms of the extremes of self-sacrifice.

Louis XV loved Jeanne Antoinette Poisson to her death. He gave her many names, among them *mistresse* and *madame* and *marquise,* but it seems she always preferred *poisson,* which meant fish and which she had received from her father, an untitled merchant in the upper tier of the third estate.

Louis first seduced her disguised as a yew tree among yew trees dancing through the Hall of Mirrors at Christmastime. To be seduced by a king of France was to sign and see signed documents that made your husband rich enough and titled enough that the king could be permitted to know you in public. A woman who ran one of the most highly regarded literary salons in Paris knew what was coming, and chose for her costume Diana, Goddess of the Hunt. The *Bal des Ifs,* as it came to be known, was like a wedding made out of whispers. After, the king went to battle Austria, and she spent months learning the accents and nods and titles and corsets that were part of the duties of a woman in her position. She learned how to address differently a duchess with an adequate chef from a duchess with an excellent chef.

I've heard the arc of history is long but bends toward justice. Which is another way of saying that you're going to have put up with a whole lot of bullshit.

In her favorite portrait, made by Delatour in 1788, her hand rests on a folio from the *Encyclopedia,* which her lover had banned for its seditious challenge to the principles of the divine rights of kings. To a point, it was erotic to be so provoked by a woman.

Jeanne had tried early in her career to interest his highness in her friends the writers, but they only knew how to bore and incense. She could hardly contain her disappointment at how they squandered the opportunities she tried to create for them. Once Voltaire took Louis by the sleeve (the sleeve!) to tell him something. Once Voltaire insisted the privies in his apartment at Versailles have doors put on them. Once after a performance of his opera on the victory at Fontenoy, he asked of the king, "Is Trajan pleased?"

And then there was Diderot. In the article in his *Encyclopedia* on "Political Authority," credit is given not to God or heritage, but to the people and their natural rights. In "Economic Politics" he lectures, "When the means of growing rich is divided between a greater number of citizens, wealth will also be more evenly distributed; extreme poverty and extreme wealth would also be rare." What more could the official royal consort do after that but turn the king's eye instead toward architecture and the stage and try to keep it there for the next twenty years?

Jeanne described herself as cold by nature. She was terrified the king might find out and tried to work herself up for his ardors using every known means. Her friends worried over the effects of so many dubious concoctions and elixirs. For a time she subsisted on a diet of nothing but vanilla, truffles, and celery. That she was always ill was a secret she kept well.

I ascribe to a brand of feminism I like to call You Don't Know Me. It's the wave that waved right after or maybe just before You're Not the Boss of Me. I have to remind myself Jeanne Poisson didn't know what her end game was either.

There were many who hated her and feared her for the control they thought she wielded. They called her a spendthrift and a whore.

"It is curious," the Duc de Nivernois said at one of the little salons she organized now in her apartment in the king's attic at the top of the king's secret staircase for the entertainment of the king himself. "We amuse ourselves in killing a partridge at Versailles, and sometimes killing men, and getting killed at the front, without knowing precisely how the killing is done." This according to Voltaire, who was not there but heard of the evening third-hand. A writer in an Age of Enlightenment couldn't risk ignoring the gossip from court if he wanted to keep his head and his wits about him. To hear him tell it, this remark was how Nivernois skillfully incited that little debate about the way to make gunpowder—equal parts saltpeter, sulfur, and charcoal; or one part sulfur, one part charcoal, and five parts saltpeter?

Jeanne interrupted then to exclaim, "We are all reduced to that about everything in the world. We are reduced to that about the rouge on our cheeks and the stockings on our feet." She was the only woman in the room, and she always knew which part was hers to play. She directed the king's eye to her ankle.

"It is a shame," sighed the Duc de la Vallière, in a way that could only have reminded everyone of Diderot's *Encyclopedia* locked up in some cellar of the castle. Who hadn't heard that Dennis had gone underground after his life's work was seized by armed men? Before supper was over, Louis had called for the volumes, which fourteen footmen delivered with dignity and flourish, each like a duck on a platter.

Among Voltaire's salon, the writers admired Jeanne, then missed her, then wondered who she had become after so many years in that palace of privilege. They may have heard the rumors that her private rooms in the attic were gilded all over with fish, that every document she signed included a flourish of carp. She put the fish of herself on everything, as if she was trying to remember herself and worried the effort was not working.

"Sire," she said, after they passed the evening amusing themselves with that remarkable compendium of human knowledge and achievement. "If one possesses it, one has all the wisdom of your realm."

Indeed, the *Encyclopedia* was very nearly comprehensive in its catalogue, and the entry on kings is only a few pages, hardly more than what was devoted to an ocean of ice at the end of the world or the construction of a mechanized loom. Some have said the lifting of the ban, followed by widespread printing and distribution was what undid the monarchy. To read—to even know that you could read—so much of the world, had the effect of snapping the peasants to their senses. If that is true, then Jeanne Poisson, Madame de Pampadour and the king's whore, did something extraordinary with that little jewelry box of a life she had.

WHY THE DAUPHIN
WON'T CONSUMMATE
THE MARRIAGE

It took Louis XVI seven years to consummate his marriage to Marie Antoinette, and to this day no one knows why.

Blundering? Phimosis? Moral frigidity? "Some have suggested the frenum is so short that the prepuce does not retract upon entry."

"He inserts his member, stays there for two minutes without moving, withdraws without ejaculating, and, while still erect, bids her good night."

I've been trying to be more honest lately.

Because I am lonely.

Sex was never easy for me either. I could blame the brainwashings of shame in my childhood or the unhelpful cutshots in those romantic comedies the patriarchy offers to us on platters with a flourish from its most dapper doms.

But honestly, I just blame myself.

His wife, the fourteen-year-old dauphine, complained he spent all of his days alone in his locksmith shop where she could not go to charm or enchant her fifteen-year-old husband.

"A tight prepuce, perhaps, prevents the head of the penis from being exposed."

According to the entry and adjoining diagrams on locksmithing in Diderot's *Encyclopedia*, the prince would have required the use of forge and anvil for lathe turning, spring tempering, rivet and screw making, precise fitting, and hole punching.

He did not know he would be the last king of France.

"What he does not know he has no one to ask."

The gates at Versailles had been left open for so many years, they could not be shut against the mob because of rust. Any man with a sword at his side was welcome to walk through the palace. Any woman with a proper dress could come to watch her queen eat. It was the duty of the royal family to let their people see them live.

This is the paradox of fame, right? How much would I like to be watched so closely right now by someone who just really wanted to know me?

The front plate and rim of a lock are joined with small rivets and should be so perfectly turned with a hammer that their location cannot be detected.

He had little conception of what his life might have been instead, though everyone around him, every ambassador, footman, royal physician, and Holy Roman Emperor of a brother-in-law had an idea in mind.

"He should be whipped until he discharges in anger like a donkey."

"He could not be more unlike his father and his grandfather."

The ingenuity of the locksmith is challenged by arranging the impediments or wards within the lock case.

In his mind he was small and sad. This is a common problem among men with the power to order a beheading.

He was an orphan, which is a common problem among kings.

He might have just tried to be happy with what he had. It was a lot, after all. But a locksmith knows you make a key out of what is not there, not what is.

THE INNER LIFE OF
CHARLES-HENRI SANSON

I want to believe people are different from how they seem. Certainly I am, and presumably you are too. Charles-Henri Sanson did not want to go into the family business. He wanted to become a doctor. As a teenager in boarding school, he kept his family and its fortune as secret as he could, but when his father suffered a stroke, his paternal grandmother insisted he assume the title Royal Executioner of France, the fourth in the family to do so.

At first apprenticed to his uncle, Charles-Henri assisted with the last execution in France that was done by drawing and quartering. Damiens, the mad man who had tried to assassinate Louis XV, left his cell that morning saying, "The day will be hard."

First, the court sentenced him to be tortured with red-hot pincers. The hand that held the knife was to be burned with sulphur, then molten wax, then molten lead, then boiling oil. The executioner was given a checklist of tortures to follow exactly. When the horses were harnessed and pulling but the limbs would not separate, the men in hoods had to wait for the watching judges to nod their assent that the arms and legs should be cut instead with an axe to end the condemned's suffering. This was when Uncle Nicolas faltered and the young man assumed the post. Those who were there said, "It took courage to watch the dreadful sight."

Later, as High Executioner of the First French Republic, Charles-Henri supported the adoption of the guillotine for a variety of reasons, which he outlined in a precisely written document with bullet points. (1) Men in his profession own and maintain their own equipment. (2) Multiple beheadings are too demanding for such a lightweight tool as an axe. Repair and replacement costs become prohibitive and constitute an unfair burden. (3) The physical exertion of the work is taxing and likely to result in accidents. (4) Victims are prone to resort to acts of desperation during lengthy, unpredictable procedures, putting the executioners themselves and members of the crowd in danger. From the tone of these remarks we might conclude his business was as tedious as any other bourgeois undertaking. He could just as easily have gotten his real estate license and married the first person in college who paid him any mind.

Few of his neighbors wanted to know him, but Charles-Henri had his solitary hobbies, which included continuing his study of medicine by dissecting the bodies of the executed. In this respect he was like many other renaissance men of the time who dabbled in science, anatomy, and art. Do you know Rembrandt's *The Anatomy Lesson of Dr. Nicolaes Tulp*? The corpse of a hanged man has been laid out on the table, and the gallery teems with men trying to understand what it means to be alive.

Sanson also enjoyed growing herbs for his experiments with medicinal concoctions. He played the violin and the cello with remarkable proficiency. His guillotine was built by his lifelong friend, Tobias Schmidt, who was a well-regarded maker of musical instruments and whose careful attention to craft Sanson admired.

When he was called to execute Louis XVI, it was not lost on him that his career began with the florid death of a man who tried to kill this man's grandfather. Our lives can be very long. So long, in fact, that we sometimes grow tired of them but don't know how to go back to that moment when we had the freedom to choose something different. Of course we didn't then recognize such freedom for what it was. After the king was dead, Sanson took a personal risk by issuing a statement of admiration for Louis's courage and faith up to the end.

Like himself once upon a time, his eldest son, also named Charles, had no taste for violence, so he took on the burly youngest, Gabriel, as apprentice instead. But Gabriel slipped from the scaffold while displaying a severed head to the crowd and died of a broken neck. No one has written a word I can find about how the father must have grieved. Only that another Charles Sanson was called upon to assume the family's title.

One of the younger Charles's early executions was of the queen, who stepped on his foot by mistake as she approached the block. She said, "Pardon me, sir, I did not mean to do it." To which he replied, "No Madam, pardon me."

The Reign of Terror wore on, and he began to quaver each morning as he took his cart to the prison to collect the condemned. As many as 54 to be guillotined in a day's work. A girl who looked to be about fourteen nearly broke his mind, he confessed. But another morning would come and he would steel his resolve once more.

I would like to have ended there, a little allegory about how we are more than what we seem to be. I was rooting for him all through the archives. But I'm always looking for the troubled underdog to win himself redemption, since it means there's hope for the rest of us. But I have since learned Charles-Henri ran a side business out of his garden selling elixirs mixed with fluids and other bits of the corpses he collected. The desperate and foolish would pay him a premium for the liquefied fat of a human corpse, which, he promised, would ease the pains of rheumatism. He offered buttons and locks of hair for sale as an heirloom or a curio or a fetish.

Many of us discover one day we are not the person we intended to be. We have grown old. We have made compromises. We are more fearful and weak than the selves of our youth would have thought possible. I imagined Charles-Henri Sanson was living a different life—doctor! musician!—inside the one he had. But actually he devoted every year he had to becoming exactly the person he was. And I—like you—am doing the same.

A RIGHT CROSS

By the right forming of such good crosses, to the utmost perfection human nature is capable of, because ... there cannot be a greater than a right cross or angle, formed by any two weapons.
    —Sir William Hope, from *A Few Observations Upon the Fighting for Prizes in the Bear Gardens*

In Robineau's painting of the duel, fifty-nine-year-old Chevalier d'Éon scores a hit on the younger Joseph Bologne.

In Robineau's painting of the duel, Chevalier d'Éon is wearing a wide-skirted black dress and white wig, in the fashion of all the dowagers at court.

In Robineau's painting, no one in the crowd knew with certainty whether it was true that Chevalier d'Éon had been born a daughter and raised a son. *Son* was an identity d'Éon endured for 49 years, though with merciful interludes as a spy dressed as a woman in the Russian courts. The crowd would only think they knew the truth when Chevalier d'Éon died and the king ordered an autopsy to prove he had the perfect anatomy of a man.

I started reading about French aeronauts, a great many of whom were women the onlookers called prostitutes, one day when I was sitting in a coffee shop ten miles past the Air Force base into the soybean fields of nowhere. The only coffee shop in my town, it was where the youth minister came to counsel teenage girls on virtue and teenage boys on Godly manliness. I was trying to keep my eyes on my own paper, but I couldn't help hearing "Our Lord is a jealous lover." There was a citation from scripture to go with this. The Ladies Auxiliary was at another table, noisy and cheerfully planning the spring quilt show. I don't know why I thought

41

of hot air balloons in particular, but I know why I was looking for the far horizon.

The historians have not been able to determine when Joseph Bologne, Chevalier de Saint-Georges, the great Parisian swordfighter, learned to play the violin. Early in his twenties he was a virtuoso, so it must have been when he was a child on the plantation where his mother was slave and his father was the master.

I lived in that mean little town where everyone congratulates themselves for being so happy and friendly for enough years that I came to believe and tried to accept that I was never going to meet someone who liked me again. My husband commented over dinner one night that I didn't seem to be able to finish sentences anymore. I would start a thought and just mumble into nothing after the first pause. I wasn't ready to tell him that sometimes I'd be grading papers or reading Foucault or copying and pasting a file onto a website and I'd hear the word *suicide* spoken in a flat voice at the back of my mind. Not like a threat or an invitation or even a possibility. Just a statement of a word that exists, like any of the other words that run through a mind in the course of a day. It might just as easily have been *divorce* or *run,* but it wasn't. It was *suicide,* and it made me afraid of how very small my life in the big house on seventeen acres far from anywhere except the Baptist church near the Walmart had become.

Surely there had once been people like me and they made their lives into something good and they left any children they might have had with something like happiness? The youth minister's brand of gender-normed asceticism pushed on girls who were twisting their hair around and around a single finger as they tried not to cry in front of him in this public place offended me to the point of brick-throwing rage. That I was afraid of him and everyone in that square after square of a town that loved him made it worse. I wanted to go to the courthouse or the public library and stand in front a brass-framed oil painting of someone who could make me feel not as if I could live, but as if I already did and I would again. But of course there was no such portrait to be found.

Everyone agreed d'Éon had the most perfectly androgynous face they had ever seen. There was a betting pool, but d'Éon refused to submit to any intimate examinations. Any result, the knight said, would be a humiliation, and one cannot put a price on honor.

In Robineau's painting of the duel, Joseph Bologne does not display the desperation of his poverty that year when the opera houses were closed. You would not guess, as the sword in d'Éon's wrinkled and shaking hand grazes the young fighter's smooth cheek, that it was the violin Bologne loved, though it was swordfighting he was loved for.

Unlike the treatises Bologne would have read as a teenager in the Royal Academy of Swordfighting and Horsemanship, Robineau's painting does not have fencers battling against a backdrop of smoke and fire billowing out from cities or plantations in ruins. He has instead the polite disinterested gazes of the Court.

Robineau knows a fight for sport does not end in death or injury. It is a show. Unlike Bologne's first duel, this was not a match of honor against a man who had publicly castigated him as "mulatto." The crowd's bets are not divided along the lines of partisan to or opponent of slavery. Unlike his first duel, it does not matter so much to him that he win, though in the end he always wins.

In Robineau's painting you cannot tell that Bologne and d'Éon had been friends since they shared a boarding house many years earlier, in the days when Bologne had only just become a man and d'Éon only just stopped playing the part of one. You cannot tell that Bologne likely granted the hit not out of deference to a lady, as the audience whispered back then, but as a sign of respect for an aging master's years of experience.

I have been trying to look on history with a more positive disposition. Because tragedy is easy and abundant. Surely it is possible to name your town after a person who had been a hero and then achieved great political influence without coming to realize fifty or a hundred years later that you've had a colonialist oppressor marbling your clock tower this whole time.

D'Éon was very good at pretending to smile. D'Éon was very good at pretending anything. A virtuoso of a spy. By the end, some documents suggest, d'Éon the woman everyone called a man had become a virtuoso at pretending nothing. It is an optimistic interpretation, and I like it. After all, in Robineau's painting, d'Éon owns that black dress. You cannot see the decades spent in exile for defying the king. Nor can you see that when the king finally commanded that d'Éon could be called a woman, it was only if he dressed forever more in the costume of a woman. D'Éon only won the choice by losing the choice. Which of course is how a king always likes to win.

Nor can you see that after the touch, the cross, the thrust, tomorrow, and the day after, Bologne will lead a regiment of black troops to the border to fight for the liberty and equality of the new French Republic. For a time he'll think he's about to lose his head, and when he doesn't he'll sail to Haiti with Julien Raimond, who was also born on an island to a French father and a mother of African heritage. They will bring their troops, paid for with their peculiar inheritances, to serve the slave uprising there. And when that revolution becomes a war between those who had white fathers and those who did not, Joseph Bologne will understand that it was always a lie the masters told, that fencing was the great art of using a sword scientifically. He'll return to Paris, because that was his home as much as anywhere.

This portrait of a swordfight makes me optimistic in a way little else does. What you can resist in this life, what you can overcome—it does not ever seem to be as much as you need. Bologne's compositions are mostly lost, so you cannot hear with any kind of historical accuracy the songs he once played, not even the best-loved one the ladies always requested, which was an account of a bird fluttering through the seasons. I think I can hear, though, somewhere in the far reaches of my mind, behind the words, how Bologne would have plucked and then bowed and then dragged the tune out from the strings of his violin.

Is the historical accuracy of this duel like the history of boxing and so much else? An audience of racist bigots laugh at how they made two freaks fight against each other instead of against those who deserve their blows? Probably. But that crowd is dead and we're the ones left. In Robineau's painting all we can see clearly are these two fencers, their swords crossing, the blossom of their tips grazing chest and cheek, the greatest of their age. When we gaze on it, we are the audience. If we like, we can gasp and clap and cheer for their triumph, for the kindnesses they grant each other even in battle. If there were noblemen who killed more people more often and more impressively with their weapons, they are long dead and their names forgotten.

BRIEF INTERVIEWS WITH THE ROMANTIC PAST

*"The voice of the Bird, for a Bird of the Air
shall carry the Voice."*

LOST CREEK CAVE

Feeling small and preyed upon, the quail hide their little handful bodies and call themselves like ghosts across the wheat. I'm only as here as a quail, on the blanket in the yard beside the field listening to the old folks talk.

Not even the quail are so indigenous to these mountains as they feel. When they left where they come from, they elected the owl to be their king and lead them across the water. He was so smug and self-satisfied, but when they arrived, it was he who was too weary and dropped right into the mouth of the first hawk that came to greet them. The quail scattered like children into the grass and never came out again.

All the men on this farm have killed other men, but in the distant enough past that they seem like haunted romantics as opposed to ruthless frightening. And anyway, what good does it do a quail to be frightened of the past?

Only in daylight would the last brother take me into the holler to see the cave they tried to brick up fifty years ago when they were boys and brave and throwing their jars of homebrew into the mouth to hear the breaking glass echo.

To haunt is to keep coming back, to the mind of someone or to a place. It holds in its oldest definitions the word *home*.

The quail know this story well. In the mountains from whence they followed the owl, the eyes of a quail would be dissolved in clear water for seven days, then mixed with oil and set alight in a candle. At the first flicker everyone in the room would become a vision of the devil on fire. Then a witch woman dropped in the engraved stone and the people all became invisible.

Even now, the old folks remember how a torrent of ghosts came pouring out of that cave. Pale Indian riders on horseback, they say, whooping and swinging tomahawks, firing their arrows with the stone-tipped spears. They knew these ghosts all too well, the thirteen brothers, having for years plowed up their arrowheads and their thumb-worn grinding stones, and even sometimes bits of their bones. The work of each summer had long been to plow those haunted mounds back down to fields for a herd of cows. They knew the ghosts were in their rights.

We hear the heifers low back to the quail as if each beast were a transformed maiden from another story of a different night.

Only nine of the thirteen brothers who saw the Indian Ghost Wind came back from the war alive. When the next war came, they felt they had to send their sons, and their sons felt they had to go. It is like a haunting with them.

A door into the ground had a full mouth of stones. The chink in the wall whistled out a cold breeze.

I've been writing everything they say, but quiet so they won't remember I'm here. My pen scratches a dash and they look over to see me in the moonlight and fireflies of this summer night. Quick, I drop my pebble.

THE GHOST CAVE

Brian's tired of telling me this story. "The cave is nothing," he says. "It's not important." What about when Uncle Bill dug a well and the bit disappeared into 70 feet of open air and then fell off so nobody even knows where the bottom of that chamber could be and he had to just pick a new spot to drill after that? "That had nothing to do with this cave.

"The Josephson Boys don't come into this either. They had their own piece of property back in the woods and they were going to build their own show cave. They dynamited a big hole in the ground and there really was a fantastic cave there. No one knows how they knew. But the thing had stalagmites and stalactites and the boys were in the process of exploring it and folks were even helping them chart it and coming out with awesome rocks and pictures. And then one day all of a sudden, no one was allowed to go in there anymore and very soon after they blocked it with two huge steel doors and that was it and they never explained themselves and they disappeared into themselves and started buying stuff like brand-new trucks and four-wheelers and additions on their house. A woman even came to live with them, and everybody said she was a mail-order bride. A couple times a year they'd go out to Colorado where it's legal to sell gold. And they never spoke to anyone, they just quit being here and sank into their land. Sitting on a pile of gold, you know, is something that makes people insane.

"The whole thing is lent a lot of extra credence because Gary Turner said down below those hills is the biggest vein of gold that has ever been and will ever be and the government knows it's there. It's one reason folks say the Forest Service is buying up so much land."

How would Gary Turner know this? "Well, what most people will tell you is he was a genius and he just knew things. If Gary Turner said something, it always turned out to be true. It might take ten years, but it would always come out.

"But that has nothing to do with this cave. This one was on land—I don't know who owns it anymore, but it must have been Great-Grandpa John's once, because he was down there drinking with all his brothers when the ghosts came out. And after they couldn't feel the cold wind of all those ghost horse hooves blowing on their neck anymore, they got up and bricked up the mouth of that cave tight with whatever boulders and stones they could find along the creek. I don't know why they thought it was better to lock the ghosts out into the world, but that's what they did.

"Grandpa John held onto his underground rights longer than almost anybody out there, but the depression came, and they were all living on flour and water.

"I guess it was fifty or sixty years later that I was out roaming—I was just a boy and had nothing better to do than spend a morning unpacking that cave, so I did. It wasn't any sort of cave to speak of—just a crevice really, no formations, long since dry. But when I was done, I squeezed myself inside to see how it felt and there, right by my shoulder, I saw a single bat, albino-white, rustling a little on its perch. It was the damndest thing, about the size of my palm, with a little mouse face, like a ghost all alone in there."

GARY TURNER,
HILL PROPHET

"Well the first thing to know is that nobody ever called him a hill prophet. You made that up. Yes, you did. I was telling you what he said about that gold vein running through the ridge and you said, 'He's like a hill prophet or something.'

"I don't really know his history or how he came to be or even how we're related. I just know him as an old man who lived in a trailer back in the woods and he was a doctor of chiropracting. He was really certified. He had diplomas on the walls, and he worked on everybody.

"When you pulled up to his place, he'd step out on the porch, this big old man, six feet tall, huge belly, dressed in a pair of blue coveralls and a hunting cap. He was so intimidating, scared the crap out of me really. He used to go coon hunting with Dad. He knew every holler for miles and miles, maybe even the whole county. Very knowledgeable about the land and the human body too. I guess. I only ever saw him hurt people.

"He'd work on them for hours, and they'd just cry and cry. His favorite tool was a turkey call, which looks a little like a dredle. It had a smooth, knobbly end, and he'd grind that with all his huge old man weight right into a pressure point. He'd be spinning it around and around, so hard the patient would scream, and then he'd cackle a little and say, 'Yup, it's not supposed to hurt like that. There's your problem.' And then he'd work that turkey call around all the other pressure points.

"It seemed sadistic to me, but he was a respected member of the community, and some folks went back to him week after week.

"I only went to him once, after I threw my back out putting up hay. He hurt me so much. God, I have never felt a pain like that in my life. I hope I never feel it again. And I only felt a little better, but I lied and told everybody he fixed me right up so I wouldn't have to go back.

"I hate to say he's a quack. Mom went to him for years after she fell out of the truck and had that metal plate in her back, and she swears he's a veritable holistic healer.

"One time he came out to the house looking for Dad, and after a while I wished I could get rid of him, but he just wouldn't go. He sat on the porch and chatted and chatted. That man could talk at you until you wished you were dead. Then all of a sudden he said, 'I found something I never seen before and someday I'm gonna show you. But first I want you to go off to college and get an education and then come back and I'll show you. Because I found something out there on the hill and I've never seen anything like it and I don't know what it means.' I thought that was pretty exceptional because he'd run these hills for his whole life, seventy years at least.

"So I went off like he said, but I never came back. Now he's gone too, and that is a regret I will live with for the rest of my life."

THE KNOWN WORLD

—for Old Hoffman, the ginseng poacher

Red on yellow will kill a fellow, red on black is a friend of Jack. Red on yellow, deadly fellow; red on black, venom lack. Yellow and red, you are dead; black and white, you're alright. Red next to black, venom lack; red next to yellow, run away fellow.

It is good luck to kill the first snake of spring. It is bad luck to see a snake climb a tree. It is good luck to keep a rattle in your pocket. It is bad luck to dream of a snake you let live and worse luck to tell anyone what you saw.

They are supposed to eat slugs, crickets, earthworms when young; skinks, frogs, other snakes when grown. But the story goes they milk the cows for nourishment and comfort. "In the morning a couple of our cows would come in with one quarter completely milked and on the teat was two red marks all swolled and red," the anthropologist's transcription reads.

I dreamed a snake nursed me like I dreamed before the baby in my belly was a hammerhead shark in a plastic egg from the quarter machine at Pizza Hut.

The story goes an old timer they called John Jackson, but could just as easily have been Uncle Leon or one of the Josephson Boys, had a black snake that lived in the house with him and his family. For five years he couldn't catch it to spade the head off the thing. On several occasions it cut the nipple off the baby's bottle and drank what was in there.

Clyde went out one morning to gather the eggs and a black snake in the nest as thick as his arm got wrapped around him so quick his daddy practically had to chop his own son's foot to get the neck out. I never put my hand into a nest easy again, and twice now it's been a good thing I keep my throat so laced up with snake fear.

Snakes go blind during dog days. Snakes go blind in the last of summer. A sidewinder will kill any living thing it touches. A blue racer will chase you if you run but run if you chase. A frightened snake will swallow its young.

The whip snake whips with its tail. The joint snake breaks into pieces. The hoop snake rolls. The stinging snake, the milk snake, and the thunder snake do what they do.

As cold as a snake, as crooked as a snake, as deadly poisonous, treacherous as a snake. Lower than a snake's belly, madder than snakes in haying.

Where they come from, none can say, but when you go root-digging with Chuck to get cash for gas, he'll tell you a smell of cucumbers in the leaves means there's a copperhead in there.

At the first thunder of spring, the snakes rustle forth. Put a snake in the fire, his feet will come out. Step on a snake, get boils on your fingers. Step on a snake, get sores on your feet. Sew on a Friday, snake in the house on Saturday.

Sometimes when you look across from one holler to the next you'll see the shadow of Old Hoffman digging out ginseng from under the old growth trees. What you have to know about Old Hoffman is that he's new blood and he's got no claim.

A snake with a poison sac must remove it to drink. When John Jackson was a boy, he could just as easily have been your father the boy, could just as easily have been you when he crept on one of those sidewinders and stole its little bindle. Oh, that beast went wild with anger, dashing itself like a joint snake against the rocks.

A snake won't die until the sun goes down. A snake won't die until it thunders. A snake won't die until the sun comes up. No matter how many pieces you hack it into a snake will put itself back together.

I'm new blood, which out here is the same as no blood. But my daughter is one of account. You can tell by how she came home one day from the briars with a possum skull in her hands and the milky lace of a shed skin around her neck.

The sweetest fiddle has a rattler's rattles inside. The sourest fiddle has no rattles and the wasps filled it up with mud nests and moaning. Snakes are the abiding place of the devil, you know. A man like John Jackson was when he was young and handsome fiddled me once a tune and I loved him something awful forever more.

"If I make my bed in Hell, you cannot help it, and I will have to lay on it"

—*Jesse Howard: Thy Kingdom Come*, CAM, Jan. 16-Apr. 1, 2015

After doing my time looking inward, I start to draw conclusions.

A lot of times people are boring.

This is because they aren't angry.

A person who is angry is always thinking.

It makes walking through the woods of knowing them exciting.

I told a man I like that when my own private apocalypse comes I will let him live through the fire of it and after I will have someone to hunt.

He laughed, which is how I know we are getting along.

Every last can of soup on this earth will be mine.

It will be quiet and I can say whatever I like.

I can do that now, but the apocalypse will help me remember I can.

Jesse Clyde Howard of Sorehead Hill had twenty acres in Fulton, MO.

Twenty acres isn't much in this world, but it's more than a lot.

A compound = land + patriarch + poverty.

City people in a gallery loving this folk art do not understand what they are looking at.

House-painted plywood jeremiads hanging around the perimeter of some property line are a dime a dozen.

"This is the Corner Tree to Hell's 20 acres."

"These People sneak up here when They think I am asleep."

I'm city people in a gallery.

I've known for some time I sorely need an equation for sincerity.

Lying, I read, is the consequence of not understanding the possibilities of what could happen between two people or a community of people.

I smile and lie and say nice things.

I do this after deciding I don't want to stand in the churchyard of what might happen between us.

Jesse Howard might be just such a one as these two or many people. He might be such a one as me.

"God bless the Owl that picked the Fowl and left the Bones for Old Man Howard."

I am a pot of righteous indignation for all of you.

I think there is a possibility of something in that pot and I don't expect it would be you coming to agree with me.

"The voice of the Bird, for a Bird of the Air shall carry the Voice. Ecclesiastes 10 = 20."

I think our stew is long since thick of meat.

I think I have this bowl for you.

I propose, Sincerity ≥ not giving up on the possibilities ÷ giving up entirely.

The Sameness of Days

FEBRUARY 1, 1949: At home. Creeks still up. Rained some.

FEBRUARY 2, 1949: At home. Cloudy all day. Not seen my shadow.

FEBRUARY 3, 1949: At home. Got some goat meat off Eddie Stout. It was fine.

FEBRUARY 5, 1949: At home. No one here. Howard Carr died sudden. Fairly nice day.

I like to make lists, lists of books to read, places to travel, recipes to try, things to do. A typical to-do list: yoga, write, walk dog, clean out barn. . . . Watch three hours of TV is not on these lists. Nap with a magazine on my face is not on these lists. Bicker with my husband Brian about whether or not he will go with me to one of the English Department meet-and-greets he so fervently hates is not on these lists. I do not keep a diary, only a day planner, because I prefer the possibility of the perfect day that the to-do list lays out to the diary's record of what was done and what was left unfinished. "Clean out the barn," for example, has been on a hundred different to-do lists at least, but hasn't been done since we moved here, and probably not for the half-century the property sat vacant before that either.

Where I come from, family and friends don't understand why I've chosen to live on a defunct farm a thousand miles from home where there's nothing but past. Barns are extinct where I come from, so they don't believe me when I tell them I have one. I don't always believe it either. The barn is a falling-down affair that still has the iron troughs and braces once used for milking and is overflowing with sixty years of household junk that no one wanted to burn in the barrels at the edge of the field. My husband spends much of his free time out there.

> AUGUST 9, 1950: At home. Archie took me down to hospital. Rained in eve.
> AUGUST 11, 1950: At home. Ray and Norma moved. Rained some in eve. Nice day.
> AUGUST 12, 1950: At home. Neil here awhile. A nice day.
> AUGUST 13, 1950: At home. Lizzie came home from hospital. Fine day.

In the year since we moved to this old farmhouse in Appalachian Ohio, Brian, who regularly attends country auctions and piles his wins wherever he can find space, has added to the heaps of scrap wood, storm windows, and buckets of rusty nails that came with the barn. His additions: stacks of *The Ladies Home Journal* tied together with baling twine, four broken chairs, a disassembled library card catalogue, a brass chandelier, six Bibles, O. S. McLeasson's diary, kept from 1949–1951, and a hundred other things.

The diary is black leather and smells like a damp basement. Tiny black flecks drift from the spine onto my lap whenever I open it. The clasp has fallen off, and the tiny lock and keyhole rest useless and rusting on the front cover. Inside the manufacturer promises, "Five years of your life, in written form will be your reward for keeping this book faithfully and accurately. . . . As you go along you will be able to turn aside the veil of forgetfulness, and see the events of two, three and even four years ago." O. S. McLeasson, who wrote his name on the blank line under this manifesto of memory, does not write what he plans to do with his days. He doesn't write about dreams he had or feelings or memories or people he misses. He simply writes what happened in terse sentences. Mostly what happened is that he stayed home and watched the weather.

> SEPTEMBER 26, 1950: At home. Set up new stove. Fine day, light frost.
> SEPTEMBER 27, 1950: At home. Charles and Dennis fight. John Smith died sudden around mid-nite. A nice day.
> SEPTEMBER 29, 1950: At home. Nice day.
> SEPTEMBER 30, 1950: At home. Nice day.
> OCTOBER 1, 1950: At home. A long lonesome day.

Although there are a few auctioneers in this county, Brian only attends Ottie Opperman's auctions. He has a couple reasons for this: "He's the only guy who does the old-timey auctioneer voice right. A lot of the other guys, they just talk it. *Now five. Now six.* But Ottie sings." Brian takes a breath and then shows me what he means. "*Now twenty-thirty-twenty-thirty, forty-five, forty-five, fitty dollar, fitty dollar, fitty dollar . . . Whoa mama!*" Ottie Opperman knows how an auction should be done. Also, Ottie's cheap. "When there's a lot of miscellaneous crap, they'll just put five or six boxes together and sell the whole lot for a buck."

The auctioneers call Brian Mr. Dollar Bill. When a big enough pile of worthless crap has accumulated, they call him out personally. "*Where's Mr. Dollar Bill-Dollar Bill-Dollar Bill? Can I get a one dollar-one dollar-one dollar bill from the dollar bill man?*" Brian can't resist. He tells me, "I ended up getting that journal because I bought an entire tabletop of books for a dollar. Or was that in the other bunch? Well, anyway, I bought that stuff for a dollar too."

Some of the things Brian looks for at an auction: corn knives, scythes, old jars, bell jars, mason jars, glass insulators, old metal fans that'll chop your fingers off, maps, adding machines, children's story books from back when they used to write about animals living in the country. "I look for relics," he says. "Things that didn't evolve to this time. Something that was once so useful and now nobody even knows what it is. Things that have no modern equivalent. Also, old videogames. I can make some money selling those on eBay." He keeps an eye out for typewriters, but "I usually lose the Underwoods. You can win anything else, but people hear the name Underwood and it's over." He's also on the lookout for a good pitchfork. "Last time I lost a pitchfork to an Amish guy. Bastard. I almost had it. It had eight prongs. Usually you get a six-prong pitchfork, or even just four. Eight is really rare."

Recently I came home late from a poetry reading on campus. A wine and cheese reception followed, and I spent an hour talking about Derrida, difficult students, a friend's divorce. It was one of those events where I was surrounded by people but felt myself sinking into loneliness. When I got home, I kissed Brian on the cheek and poured another drink. "How was the reading?" he asked. I raised my glass. "I'd like to make love to you, but I'm going to finish this first."

When I married Brian, I married three hundred acres on an Ozark hill and the underground rights his great-grandfather sold to Doe-Run, I married the brittle corn, the August droughts, an artesian spring Doe-Run sank, a hundred head of parched cattle trucked in the end down a gravel

road, his father down that road, himself on a motorcycle thinking some-
how he could go back some day.

I brought the city into our marriage. I brought too many lights, too
much noise, the chatter of people, the clink of glasses, the clink of money,
the click of polished shoes on travertine tile, and always, somewhere in
the distance, a moaning siren.

Still, I think things are working out pretty well. One reason is I sometimes come home late to find all the lights off and Brian sitting on the
couch in sweatpants and no shirt looking like—well, an auctioneer might
say "wild-eyed as a raccoon on a raft." I pour my wine and make my
propositions, and Brian, who is leaning against the sink with his arms
folded across his bare chest, says, "No thanks. I feel weird." I feel weird
too.

JULY 8, 1951: At home. Mowed some weeds. Fine day.
JULY 9, 1951: At home. A long lonesome day. Nora Atwood funeral.
JULY 14, 1951: At home. Norma brought over some beets and carrots.
JULY 16, 1951: At home. No one here. A long day.

Brian is a man who courts melancholy. Ways he does this include:
standing in the woods in the rain listening to the wind, playing Chopin's
nocturnes in a dark, empty house while thinking about his lost childhood,
reading page after page of a dead man's journal in a crumbling barn. But
he doesn't tell me about the journal right away. Instead he asks why I
have to drink in order to be with him. He asks if I'm really so unhappy,
if he's really so undesirable. When I ask, "What's wrong with you?" he
shuffles out of the room without saying a word.

Between a few pages of the diary an extra note is taped in. July 31,
1951 is one of these days:

George Wend—died
Tom Davidson"
Dale Smith killed in Germany
J. E. McCormack died
Mrs. Alice Grayes died
Elyse Barton died

Eighty pages later the journal ends. October 21, 1951: At home.
Two other sentences have been erased and only the illegible shadow of a
thought remains.

Because the only people he mentions are those who intermittently visit, I imagine O. S. McLeasson died alone. I imagine Norma or Archie, Charles or Dennis came by days later with some squirrel meat and found their neighbor dead on the floor, a jar of hickory nuts spilling out from his hand.

We've made a lot of deals in our marriage: A couple years in the metropolis for me, then the Bitterroot Mountains for him. Appalachia sits in the middle of the places we each want to be. My Moroccan lanterns hang from the window, he keeps a closet full of hay knives. I buy a moccha-chino every day in town in exchange for watching after eight laying hens on a farm twenty miles out. Take out the garbage, and I'll go to the party alone.

On this particular night Brian is not in the mood for deals. "I'm going to bed," he says.

"Wait." I grab his wrist tight. "Don't."

I set my glass on the coffee table and pull him back to the couch. *The Daily Show* is on TV. I put my head on his chest and wrap my legs around his legs. He tucks a blanket around both of us, and we fall asleep this way.

SEPTEMBER 14, 1951: At home. No one here. Nice day.

SEPTEMBER 15, 1951: Sat at home. William brought some groceries. Fine day. Squirrel time.

SEPTEMBER 17, 1951: At home. Clyde gave us some sweet corn. Might be our last sweet corn. Fine day.

SEPTEMBER 18, 1951: At home. Clyde gave us another mess of corn. A beautiful day.

ABIDING

When I married him, there were things I thought were jokes that were not jokes. In thirteen years I have often changed my mind about which are which.

"A Blair will sooner knife you than shoot you," the old timers say with a laugh and serious eyes that hold your face longer than you would like.

He is an atheist who believes in haints and the resurrection of the body, and when he dies, he wants his remains left in the holler beside the foundation of the cabin where the first Blair was born. He's upset about how there are no wolves or bears left on that fifty acres to render his body. It's one of the things about neighbors you have to abide.

He has kin he won't claim living out on Monkey Mountain Road and uncles with show caves and cousins with haints and criminal records, a grandpa with one eye who drinks and who everyone calls crazy.

There is a code about family and what you do for them, which is anything, and everyone else, to whom you owe nothing, and whose living gets in the way of your living, but they also have family who would do anything, so you abide each other as best you are able.

He does not want his organs donated. He says, "I don't want to find out later that I need them."

I didn't take his name, but I have his power of attorney, so I thought it right to tell him I would feel a moral obligation to donate his organs despite his wishes. I told him this so he could make someone else legally responsible if it matters so much. It was a question of conscience for me, it was my code.

His code does not abide other codes. "I have taken many of your responsibilities off your plate. Our daughter carries the name. My father will take care of my body." As long as his father doesn't die and his daughter stays obedient, I won't have to think about getting my hands corpse-dirty or shovel-blistered, or contemplate jail time for illegally dumping remains. So I think about neighbors who need organs instead.

Then he's not mad anymore and he says, "Nevermind. I'll just make sure I take you with me."

I've asked him in my most serious voice not to threaten to kill me anymore, because I can't tell what parts are kidding.

"Death," he says, "is a gift." He won't squander it on anything less than a boat full of fertilizer somewhere along the Colorado. Is that a joke?

Is it a joke that I will be tied to the mast?

It is most likely a joke and well delivered and hilarious.

When we were dating he talked about how much he wanted to jump a train and tramp. We were reading so many books together I thought we were having a different conversation. We made up hobo names and I chose Marge because that's a name that is also a funny sound.

He chose Head-in-a-Bag Hobo because he was starting to realize he'd never have it in himself to vanish as long as I was alive, but in grief he'd be unable to hold himself back. When he left, he'd carry my shrunken head with him in his bindle to be his love and his weapon against the bulls and other murderous insane hobos in the yards.

I thought he was so funny and romantic.

There was a year we were living on seventeen acres in Ohio, and every six hours or so a train skirted the edge of the field. When I was pregnant we sat on the trellis bridge and skittered stones across the frozen creek while we picked names and listened for a distant whistle.

When the baby was gone, I sat at the window and watched the wind blow the grass and for months it's the only thing I remember. But he remembers that he had finally worked up the nerve to go, and I held his hand and cried and said, "Please, I can't lose you too." So he didn't go. And now we have a living child whose name is Blair, and if I die, he'll take her along, and if I don't, his whole life will be something different. He promises he can abide that because we are family.

This means I should put his whole body in the woods for the wolves that will never come. That I should stop thinking about mothers on dialysis and children who have gone blind and how a heart falters into the straightest green line you've ever seen.

I thought Blair was something I was becoming and he did too, but when we're being honest it's clear I have no honor and he tells no jokes. We're right to fear each other.

IN A TIME OF DROUGHT

More practical men turn their attention to the apple. More desperate shake the persimmon. For luck, look to the plum.

A water witch is an old man or an old woman or a young man or a young woman or a child or a virgin or not. This one picked up a bough and she couldn't tell you why her hand shakes.

This one used to be a long-haul trucker and now he witches and the money's the same. This one prefers a willow switch, but always peach in a drought. This one won't tell you why the trunk is studded with nail and nail and nail.

A peach wants the bruise of a frost and batter of drought to feel desperate and fruiting. A good year for peaches is a good year for tomatoes is failure for corn is a famine for potatoes.

Sometimes a peach tree feels the working of hands with ladders, and sometimes it feels the immortals who live inside its dream opening cabinets to clatter the juice glasses.

There once was a woman looking everywhere for her ladder to look for a child she wanted so desperately she couldn't think to hem or plough or hew a rod to witch. The ladder was sideways beneath the yellow grass in the orchard.

A boy who lived in the dream of the peach tree consented to be a son and climbed down from the river of heaven. Rain is how when we sleep in the nest of the inside of my elbow, we are boughs witching toward the welling. Rain is how he does not know and how he sometimes asks, *What peaches, Mama? What peaches?*

SHORT TREATISE ON
THOSE ANIMALS
WHICH WEAR CLOTHES AND
THOSE WHICH DO NOT

Hitty Pitty within the wall, Hitty Pitty without the wall.
If you touch Hitty Pitty, Hitty Pitty will bite you.

Nutkin taunts Old Brown, the owl in shadow, for no apparent reason, except a squirrel cannot stand subservience, except an owl is death and a squirrel is not.

Because I liked him so much for riddling the unflappable owl day after day, I begged him, Nutkin, please, tuck your tail under your knees.

The only squirrels I had known were dead beside the road.

Once I ran over something small and bushy-tailed, and it was one of the truly terrible nights of my life. A grief of headlights and the most ordinary of things that happens to everybody.

It was 27 miles every day down Highway 13. Another time I had a miscarriage on the way home and drove the stretch of it after sometimes but not always remembering.

All of the squirrels are naked, but Old Brown wears a waistcoat.

Sooner or later Nutkin winds up in that pocket.

Once I knew a squirrel a little, when my daughter was learning to walk and she had an idea she could catch it. He flirted with her, and I thought he must be the most benevolent and generous of creatures to be playing with my baby in the grass. When his nails made busy clicks on the brick path, it reminded me of how Coleridge said fancy takes you out of your life, but imagination brings you more deeply into it.

If you read about neonatal development as you go, it's like watching a fish crawl onto land, grow fur, drop its tail and build a fire. One of the times I was pregnant—I can't remember which anymore—I felt like I was gestating a frantic and skittering chipmunk. Is this fancy or imagination?

Some grown-up experts on children will tell you anything less than nonfiction is a mean joke to play on people who cannot distinguish reality from fantasy, and some will tell you nonfiction is a mean joke to play on people living in the dreamscape of an undeveloped id. These experts will find agreement only on the subject of animals behaving like small people, which, they say, insults the dignity of animals and children alike.

When I was a girl, I loved this story, as my daughter loves this story. Now I love it even more.

Nutkin spent his days arranging the thorns into rows and figures atop the wall, always keeping his eye on the closed door of that tree.

I had to pull the car over and try to breathe. It hurt so much and there was blood on my legs. Later I'd be driving into town and pull off at the same shoulder to nurse in the back seat.

The fields on the side of the road were full of thistles, purple and round as stars.

If you move very carefully, hitty pitty, you can cut the stalk and peel back the prickle skin. Beneath there is a kind of green milk that is sweet.

When the time came, there was a flutterment and a scufflement, but out popped Nutkin, tail-less and hissing. He became as dangerous as an owl, throwing pinecones at anyone who approached to offer him a riddle or a tail on a pin.

The squirrels that came after wore little jackets with buttons. Their sitting rooms overflow with quantities, and still they collect more nuts. "Imagine how hungry we'll be," they say to each other, "when we wake from the long winter." They don't know what Nutkin is about.

BESET UPON ALL SIDES

In my facsimile edition of *The Book of Deer*, a tenth-century Latin gospel illuminated in the Scottish lowlands, the monks peopling the margins have doe eyes and hooves. Abbot-fawns, they speak in the cursive script of deer bodies blowing fanfare out their snouts. Sometimes the mouth of an abbot is the m-silhouette of a bird flying away.

When I was a monk using my hoof hands to copy out "The Apostles Creed," I told myself every hour, "I chose this, I chose this, I'm choosing this, I chose this."

Then I would think about beautiful Saint Teresa, naked and flagellated at the center of Rome, until it occurred to me *Lives of the Saints* is pornography. "The self-surrender may become so passionate as to turn into self-immolation. It may then so overrule the ordinary inhibitions of the flesh that the saint finds positive pleasure in sacrifice." It's like how the O that starts this book is an elongated body of a deer wrapping around itself to nuzzle the ear of an abbot straddling its neck.

The first time I saw God I was eight and he was floating on a cloud over my bed, saying, "Katie, I want you to do my will." I was marveling at how he was so fat the belly folds rolled over the edge of nimbus and made the whole thing bob like a pool raft. Then I remembered God can read minds so I started praying to myself, "Please don't think God is fat, please don't think God is fat," but it didn't work.

73

William James was the first psychiatrist to attempt to parse the difference between religious feelings and mental illness. "The sentiment of reality can indeed attach itself so strongly to our object of belief that our whole life is polarized through and through." *Varieties of Religious Experience* is over a thousand pages and has only proved I'm fortunate not to believe what I see.

St. Francis was the son of wealthy fabric merchants but gave his inheritance to the women curing indigo dye in a vat of steeping human piss. He threw his cloak at the feet of his weeping mother and walked naked through the streets. When Sister Leona decided not to turn the TV around, but let us watch every muscle of his buttocks clench as he stretched his arms out before the woods at the edge of town, welcoming himself into God's embrace, I knew I was a sinner not to shuck off my red wool sweater and plaid jumper to march barefoot down Flad Avenue, under the overpass, and into whatever was on the other side of Salamma's liquor store and convenience mart.

That night when I was a virgin, God was an obese man in swim trunks and sexy, if you like men you have to climb, which I do. I looked great in a sarong. We had sex on the sand beneath a full white moon and afterward, for once, he didn't ask me for anything.

Now I keep a garden because God likes self-reliance. I spent $700 on a deer fence because God sends mixed messages. Every night raccoons and groundhogs chew through the bottom of the mesh. Rabbits follow at dawn, eating everything down to nothing. When I live-trap a raccoon, I set it free on the other side of town, which is illegal and un-neighborly. I know the right thing to do, but I don't have the stomach to do it.

Saint Anthony was assailed by howling lions storming the breaches of his mountain fortress. If you let yourself listen, he preached through a vow of silence, a cave opens up in your sternum, and in there grows a blossom of brimstone.

You can put this flower in your rifle and smite the vermin, can you not?

"When the outward battle is lost, and the outer world disowns him, it redeems and vivifies an interior world which would otherwise be an empty waste."

The groundhog is in the crosshairs. I've only fired a gun once, and it was into a tin can on a fence post one Christmas morning. I know there is no God, but if there is, he's always telling me these funny stories. I think I like that guy. Maybe we're falling in love.

FRED SANDBACK
MAKES ME MISS THAT
TEENAGE FEELING

Fred Sandback makes forms subtly calibrated to the architectronics of space.

Apprehension of a work by Fred Sandback involves kinesthetic viewing to appreciate such valorized examples of logistical ephemera.

Fred Sandback's works are without insides.

I was a teenager in a gallery at the Forum for Contemporary Art. There were other teenagers and a grant to art us out of the inner city.

The gallery was white, naturally, except where Fred Sandback had affixed black strings and also where those strings cast bluish shadows.

Just trying to remember myself then, I feel wrapped up in those aggressively white walls. Like the worst of something. Like when a person walks into a room where there's just you and then that person turns around immediately without saying anything and walks back out.

I wore a plaid uniform every day of my life. I had to smoke pot for years before I stopped wearing that culotte in my dreams. Those deliberate fibers, those tethered wonders of fragility and force, "Fuck them," I think whenever I see myself wearing a blue button-up shirt in the mirror.

In the gallery, the pieces are coexistent with, as opposed to overwhelming, the environment.

The wall is a pivot. The strings are vectors skimming the air.

I learned Fred Sandback's name only after he killed himself and the newspaper ran an appreciation. What a surprise, the yarn guy was a very important person in certain circles.

There were just enough strings to make a triangle in one corner, a trapezoid in the other, and a rectangle within the white rectangle of wall. It seemed like the point of the show was to illustrate how perfectly void the gallery was, and also how the curator only wore black and used a lot of foundation to make herself seem very pale.

One of the teenagers in the gallery was Adam, who went to the alternative high school, where all the kids were on drugs I'd heard. Adam was on drugs. He had many piercings and a skateboard and no one dropped him off—he appeared, as if by bus or some other miracle, as if he were an emanation of the city itself.

A Sandback creates oppositions to the illusions of oppositions. You are what you say you are not.

Every Saturday I emerged out of my mother's Corolla. It occurs to me now that I could have asked her to drop me off down the block and then no one would have known what corner of the bourgeois I emanated from.

I had a fantasy that Adam would kiss me. Him or someone else. I tried pretending to want to skateboard, because maybe skateboarding would turn into heavy petting. He kicked his board to me, and the rolling echo filled the emptiness of the room. I stood on it, then fell. The skateboard slid, slow like someone was bending the fabric of time, into one of the ephemeral strings, which silently slipped out of the wall.

The ragged thread spun a little cyclone under the air vent. We watched it and felt how the end of the triangle didn't change a single thing about the space in the room. Which, of course, changed the space in the room.

The curator rushed to jam it back into the nail hole before anyone saw. I said I was sorry, but I wasn't. It was the stupidest art I had ever seen. It didn't even get me to first base.

Fred Sandback would probably consider the incident with the skateboard an engagement with the local nuances of phenomenological experience. He's probably a good-natured guy, lying in his grave, not rolling over to hear me to tell this story. Which is disappointing, because surely there are some things that can't be made right.

To experience a Sandback is to brush with temporality, seriality, and change.

Fred Sandback simultaneously entices and denies the haptic.

In a room with his strings nothing is tangential except the lines to the air, which thrill, little teases.

DMV & FLEDGLING

I was first in line outside the locked door of the DMV, leaning against a granite planter with no plants but many cigarette butts, reading a book about an 1850s plantation to pass the time. Near my feet, I was startled to notice, a pink slug of flesh oozed itself along the sidewalk mysteriously until I understood this was a baby bird, featherless and facedown, breathing desperate breaths of an expanding and contracting rump. The July sun had just crowned itself into a direct line on its body, which looked more like scar tissue than it did something new and becoming. I couldn't see a nest, but there was a drainpipe too high to reach that maybe was stuffed full of yellow grass and gum wrappers.

I asked the man in line behind me if he thought there was anything to be done, and we both agreed there was not. More people arrived to wait beside the locked door and watch a fledgling dying on the sun-baked concrete at our feet, and I was reminded again of how frightening bureaucrats and functionaries can be.

Only yesterday I got pulled over in a town that rose out of the corn and soybean fields because the tags on my car were expired. I had new ones in my glovebox, but it was raining when I got them, and I never remembered to stick them on. Then, in the pile of year after year of proofs of insurance and receipts from Wendy's, I could not seem to find them or an up-to-date insurance card, and I never did bother to get a new driver's license when we moved here because of how hard-won that still-fresh Ohio one was.

In Ohio I stood in a line at the DMV pushing my not even a month-old baby back and forth in a stroller while no one looked at anyone else, then nursed her under a blanket while I stood on the linoleum so I wouldn't lose my two hours invested in that line. Every so often a shadow would pass in the corner of the room, and I'd have to grab the handles of the stroller tight for balance until the light came back again. I wouldn't know for another two days that I was hemorrhaging and infected, that I would need surgery and to be in the hospital for three nights pumping through the sweats of a serious fever to make little desperate bottles of breast milk for my baby at home. The cord for the pump was often tangled in the IV to my arm. A nurse who questioned whether this milk was safe took it upon herself to pour every bottle down the drain while I slept, and when the lactation expert from the city hospital called down to this remote province to say my milk, at least, was perfectly fine, it couldn't be unpoured.

At home, where the baby was without me, I thought I could hear my sister pulling back the foil on a tin of powder. For ten years I didn't eat anything from Nestle because of how they sent representatives to underdeveloped countries to tell women that formula was best for babies, which they knew was untrue and knew would drive families deeper into poverty trying to buy such a promise, and when wars came or coups or famine, the people from Nestle were gone, their powder scarce, water not safe to drink, and you would hear starving cries in the back of the radio while reporters clucked their tongues.

But now my child is four and my uterus is tucked back in where it should be. I haven't felt myself waver as a blood clot gasped loose of me in years. We drive to the park together chatting without a care, and when the blue lights come on, I reach around to the back seat to touch her thigh and say, "Don't be nervous, honey. Policemen are helpers." And it's true he doesn't seem like a threatening person—despite the egregious state of my paperwork, he doesn't even give me a ticket. Instead he says in the condescending way of an absolute authority who wants to be liked, "You don't want a ticket today, do you, ma'am?" But really, I do. I prefer a simple exchange of predetermined penalty for obvious infraction to the uncertainties surrounding a police officer who has decided to be nice. "No officer, I do not want a ticket," I say in the softest and most demure voice I can manage, not because I mean to be manipulative with my womanly wiles, but because I can't seem to stop myself from adopting this submissive stance when I'm afraid. And I'm afraid if I don't play the part quivering, there is no script for this encounter at all.

I want him to just hand me the ticket—my paperwork is not in order so I must submit more paperwork, and one of these pieces of paper would be a check it would pain me to write but that is the consequence. Instead I'm buckled into my seat rambling about how "My husband usually takes care of these things" and "I'm so nervous I can't remember my own zip code." And he is charmed by all of it, smiling like someone who enjoys feeling kind to say, "I'll let you off today with a warning." He's smiling to turn his eyes on my daughter in her carseat, who is trying hard to be brave and not cry while he says, "You keep that seatbelt buckled now, you hear." And maybe it's not true of this particular cop, but I suspect it is true even of this particular cop, that if I were not a combination of white and middle class and demure and mother, the exchange would have been quite different, which is one more reason I would have preferred the simplicity of law.

My child is so grown now I can leave her under the eyes of some other adult while I spend an entire morning at the DMV. For a while I sat in my car in the parking lot outside the locked building listening to the radio and enjoying the solitude. In Syria and Iraq, I hear, the governments of towns and even mid-sized cities are being slung back and forth like machine guns over a shoulder. I always think about the mothers first. When you have a child in your arms, you only want a few simple things. This is why breastfeeding made me a little less afraid and why I hated that half-full can of formula in our cabinets. It was like a threat of need. Now that I have a pair of free hands, I can think again about ideology and ambition and which side I would take and which government supplied those guns.

While I made my body into a tree over the bird, I thought about how many of us might be so raw and pink as this in our lives. How easy it might be to wake up one morning in a line while CNN runs the footage of your baby crying just behind another middle-aged man in a crisp new tactical vest talking into a microphone. In my shadow the bird began to lift its head and strain. One way of looking at it was that the bird was more comfortable and better able to move in the shade, could even muster the strength to try flapping its wings. Another way to interpret these actions was that my shadow had just amplified its terror.

What would someone with my hugeness and power be able to do for someone so small and suffering? A grocery ad, bigger than the newspaper it fell from, had blown under the concrete planter, and I used this to scoop up the bird and carry it to a grassy lawn under a tree at the far side of the parking lot. There were cigarette butts there too. The grass was wet with dew and maybe the bird would be shivering cold now and raptors would not hesitate to dive down and take its throat at this distance. So there was little by way of favor about my gesture, but I knew I would prefer to face my death in the shade of grass over the hot sidewalk beside the DMV, so I gave this preference to what I could not understand and hoped it was good.

When I came back to the line, everyone had been let inside to make new lines, and though every person there had gazed upon the bird themselves and watched me slide it onto the paper and all said "poor thing" with sad voices as I carried it away, they did not offer me back my place at the front. Their refusal to even make eye contact suggested I should be grateful that every one of these obedient citizens had been so good as to leave my purse alone and unrifled on the sidewalk.

I do not wish to be small-minded. It was my privilege to be allowed so near as to see the shadows of bones through a fledgling's translucent skin as it tried to make those wings work. It was my privilege to know a bird in this intimate way. I hope it did not feel as if I carried it even farther from its mother's reach. I hope it did not feel the dewy grass compounded its miseries. Bureaucrats and functionaries, if it is me, do not hesitate to move my body to a spot you would not mind laying on, wherever it may be. If that is as much as can be done for me, do that much, and if I were you, when I returned from the interruption of such a moment, I would demand back my place and cry shame on those who shuffled ahead while matters of heat and breath unfolded beneath your thinking what good could possibly be done. You are the first of the day to have a license moved from one state to another. You are not the third. The bird will not live. You will sign your name first, as is fair and just and right.

CHRISTMAS NIGHT

The morning I was reading the Russian poet Anna Akhmatova who said of the terrible years of the Yezhov Terror when she spent seventeen months in the prison lines in Leningrad, "I was with my people then, / there, where my people unfortunately were" was the same morning I was listening to the news about the use of chemical weapons on a village in Syria. We're not at war with Syria, you could say, but most people were saying, "We're not at war with Syria yet."

A lot of what I know about Syria I picked up from a relation of mine in the Secret Service who did one of his hardship tours there and says to this day it was his favorite country because of the kindness and hospitality of the people. His brick walk-up is filled with brass heirlooms and rugs from Damascus. His position is not as romantic as a post at the White House, but Dick Cheney once gave him a pin at Christmas and it meant a lot to him because he really liked Dick Cheney. He said no one treats guys like him better. I have a hard time reconciling that with my political ideology, but I try. I try not to file it away in the category "Banality of Evil" because how you treat people who serve you and under you is important and not just a decoration of personality.

So Dick Cheney is good to the people he meets.

I used to write polemics for leftwing newspapers we printed at Kinko's when we could raise the money. Dick Cheney is one of the people I did not hesitate to call evil.

I still think it is his fault a lot of people died, and *a lot* means not a number you can count, but at least 919,967. Mercifully it is not a number that includes my cousin who did two tours in Afghanistan. One Christmas in the middle of it, he was on Skype telling about last night's duty with an Afghani soldier, and because of how the hand-off was going, my cousin was armed and the Afghani was not, but Jesus Christ, for the last week now guys had been attacked in the night by monkeys. Actual goddamn primates that get on your face and fuck you up.

My cousin and his mom lived with us for a while when things got bad, and I've always thought that makes him my brother. When he was sixteen, he came to visit me on campus and we got stoned together and went to see the Tibetan monks making a sand painting in the Anthropology Department. He agreed it was totally like the green sand they tapped out of their spoons turned into a blossoming morning glory right in front of our eyes. Not long after he was expelled from high school and in rehab and then living out of his car and then he was just missing and then Army, if he could get his juvie record cleared up, which he could because everyone who signed up then knew where they were going. What he said to me before he left was "If somebody's got to die for this, it should be somebody like me."

He was wrong about that of course. Just one reason he is wrong is that, against regulations, he gave an Afghani national his knife because he thinks nobody should have to stand in the dark next to an American with a rifle waiting to get his face ripped off by a macaque.

What I wish is that we were kids again and he's pretending to be an alligator like he always did while I pretend to be a wild warrior queen and we're in the treehouse eating Barbie legs, which we pretend are hot dogs, and I wish I wasn't crying about my poor beautiful Barbies and that instead of getting him in deep shit with my mom I'm sitting down next to him, chewing on that dismembered beige plastic as we tell each other how delicious it is. I wish my Facebook status wasn't a meme with a Gandhi quote, and I wish his wasn't a picture of the son he hasn't seen in the year since he deployed.

Another cousin joined up too after the housing bubble burst and he couldn't find work. He was done with Basic and didn't know where he was going next, but since the surge had come and gone, Okinawa was most likely. My grandfather raised a glass to the hero in the family. I really can't stand that naïve and pandering line of bull, but later, after more drinks, my grandfather will tell how in 1945 his platoon set sail at night, ground forces bound for the Pacific front and the bomb hadn't been dropped yet, so they didn't know they wouldn't have to be heroes. He'll tell how it was so dark they thought they were sailing straight into the end of the world. He could cry for his mother and no one would know, it was so dark, the sea and the sky.

When they finally landed in Korea, everything was different and it was his job, he said, to guard the perimeter and shoot at those poor bastard communists starving as they tried to steal food from the trash. His eyes are watching them even now.

When it's Christmas night and my relation in the Secret Service wants to lighten my grandfather's mood, he tells stories about famous people he has watched. When he was guarding the Dalai Lama at a ball game, his holiness saw him smiling behind his dark glasses to see the Cardinals make an RBI and asked him to sit down and explain the game. He and the Dalai Lama talked ball for an inning, and apparently the Dalai Lama is a real stand-up guy. The stars were shining over the moths crackling in the stadium lights, and to hear this man describe how carefully he filled in the boxes of a scorecard reminds me of how the monks in their robes were like red and yellow birds darting among the trees as they poured all of those lacings of sand into the creek, and I was there then where my cousin was and he was there with me.

WITH OR WITHOUT YOU

On a scale of 1–10, how would you rate your overall happiness? I rest at a 7. Though I often think it's preposterous to tell yourself you can live within rounding of 10. I'm really a 6, but telling myself the truth of that makes me so much a 4 that I just lie and say 7, knowing 6 is in there.

Yesterday driving home and listening to the radio play some old song I've always liked—this was after the talk radio hour on the metaphysics of time—I thought I might be turning into an 8. But 8 is such a silly, laughable state of joy. You can only survive 8 for about a day. So I'll say 7, but my 7 lately is swelled up with 8 wrapping her big arms around 6 and kissing him on the top of the head.

Old people apparently are happy and get happier the older they get. Sociologists call it the paradox of aging. And no, it's not dementia— researchers solved for that variable and found the more clear-minded you are, the more likely you'll exhibit the paradox. The researcher being interviewed hypothesizes that being released from the burden of the future is what does it.

This past weekend at the Chinese Lantern show at the Botanical Garden we had to get my grandmother a wheelchair because the darkness of the night and her blindness made it too much for her to go on. But oh she didn't want to get in that chair. She sat on a bench by the fountains for a long time. And when it was time to go, I asked her to please use the wheelchair for us. Manipulative, but helpful I hoped. She wanted my daughter to ride in her lap, and I loved her so much for how she never gives herself up.

But my little daughter is a very heavy person now, especially for the lap of an 89-year-old woman feeling faint. I carried my girl to the car when she asked, even though my dad was right to say that she's big enough to walk. "It won't be much longer now that I'll be able to carry her like this," I told him. "It's nice how her head feels on my shoulder." And of course he knows something about that.

Grandma, once she was finally sitting in the wheelchair said, "Well, it's done now. A first time for everything." I hadn't realized she'd never before had to admit she couldn't go on. Then she laughed and said, "I'll have to tell Tiny."

Tiny is her best friend and is 91. They met at the senior citizens center in a chair yoga class and are in agreement that the Tai Chi instructor is no good—they're too old to be told to hold their elbows in now. So when Tiny had to pick a nursing home, she picked my grandmother's and they sit together at every meal and tease the woman at their table who collects cracker packages and can't work her toaster. How surprising to make a best friend at this age—or maybe how natural.

Eighty years ago Tiny was a child being raised in an orphanage after her mother died and her father gave up, and even now there's so much of that in her. Perhaps, my grandmother thinks, because a nursing home is a lot like an orphanage. You should see how Tiny cleans, how bothered she gets to clean even when she can't really bend down to manage it. And then my sweet grandma laughs and says, "But of course there's something wrong with all of us or we wouldn't be here." She's thinking of how she can't really see anymore, just fogs and light and her optic nerve concocts visual hallucinations out of its starvation so much of the time she sees her mother's cousin sitting off to the side of the room in a green dress. She ignores her mostly but sometimes thinks it would be nice if that woman really were the angel she thought she was seeing at first, instead of an ordinary medical condition.

Every ten years the happiness researchers at Harvard give their subjects a personality profile, and every time the subjects are astonished at how much they changed over the past decade, and every time they grossly underestimate how much they'll change before the next decade is out. It makes people happy, the scientist hypothesized, to think you've become the person you were meant to be.

It makes me happy to think I'll never be done becoming, but I'm sort of a freak I guess. It doesn't make sense that I should be to me, but I've observed I seldom agree with others on matters of happiness. No one I talk with thinks 6–8 is the most ideal range, far superior to 8–10.

I forgot to mention, old people's happiness is not composed of more happy moments, but fewer sad moments. Also, the happy moments become more complicated, containing mixtures of positive and negative feeling.

Also, I spent years trying to train myself to be a Buddhist, which was miserable, shrinking into the box of just this moment, with no ranging mind running its fingers through the timeline of its making and becoming. But I try to believe in the wisdom of people happier than I am and who speak to the collective experience instead of via the individualized narcissism of the personal essay.

Then this from one of the scientists: Of the past, present, and future, the present is the least real. Like the shore, which is nothing. There is no line between sand and water, only sand, only water.

How happy to be freed from zen and the art of flagellating my wandering mind.

I wish you could have seen the light on the bluffs alongside I-70 last night. It's been the wettest summer I can remember, so the grass is misty almost with the sway of its own tassels and wild roses and various yellow daisy things freckle the vista of the valley pouring itself into the Little Laramine River. It was raining all afternoon, it will rain again when that ashen storm cloud passing out of the west arrives, so the night rises from the hills and the dampness glows it back on itself, making this rosy hour.

The song that's playing now, as I drive home to kiss the people I love who thought of me intermittently throughout this day, the song is one I loved when I was fifteen and copying lyrics in my notebook, learning how nice a little sadness can be. Enough decades have passed that I feel more like the blind woman in the wheelchair I will become than the girl I once was.

But of course I'll be so surprised. It will be a second or a feeling. How strange, the way it will hold an entire life inside it, a moment, over before it even happened. Look at the pretty thing, fluttering itself off over the flowers.

ACKNOWLEDGMENTS

This book is for my parents. I owe a great debt to my oldest and dearest friends, Peter Nuernberger and Sam Nuernberger, who make the past seem wonderful strange enough to write about.

This book wouldn't have happened without Brian Blair, who told me so many of the stories first, edited the ones he didn't tell, and always raises his hand when I am in need of a villain or strawman. I am also grateful to the rest of my Blair family: Pam Blair, Norris Blair, Carey Rulo, and Chuck Rulo who reiterate, supplement, embellish, and contradict all accounts. In loving memory of Nadine Blair, who always told the one about the penny.

Many thanks to those who gave me feedback on and ideas for the essays in this book, especially Rose Gubele (who taught me the term "trickster rhetoric"), Ellie Kozlowski, Kathy Leicht (the great wit and satirist), Rachel Mehl, Wayne Miller, Jenny Molberg, Dinty Moore, Phong Nguyen, Sarah Nguyen, Art Ozias, Laura Read, Kat Smith, Rich Smith, Roseanne Weiss (who invited me to the art gallery a very long time ago now), Ellen Welcker, Bob Yates, and Maya Jewell Zeller. I'm also thankful for such supportive communities at Eastern Washington University, Ohio University, and the University of Central Missouri. And a great many thanks to Michelle Herman and everyone at OSU Press for generous comments and nurturing of this manuscript into book form.

Much appreciation to the editors of journals that first published the essays in this collection:

Float, Cleave, *The Journal*
"And now brightness falls from the air . . . ," *Lake Effect*
The Gazelle, *Lake Effect*
The Blue Sky, the Gray Woods, *Lake Effect*
Heed Not the Milk Hare, *Diagram*
Introduction to the Symbols of the Revolution, *Heavy Feather Review*
On Horseback, *Heavy Feather Review*
Plutarch's *Parallel Lives of Virtue and Failing*, *Heavy Feather Review*
Pantoum for Tilly Matthews, *Tupelo Quarterly*
Trinkets, *Tupelo Quarterly*
Why the Dauphin Won't Consummate the Marriage, *Tupelo Quarterly*
The Inner Life of Charles-Henri Sanson, *The Journal*
The Known World, *Sundog Lit*
"If I make my bed in Hell, you cannot help it, and I will have to lay on it," *Sundog Lit*
The Sameness of Days, *Redivider*
Abiding, *Iron Horse Literary Review*
In a Time of Drought, *Mid-American Review*
Short Treatise on Those Animals Which Wear Clothes and Those Which Do Not, *Defunct*
Beset Upon All Sides, *Diagram*
Fred Sandback Makes Me Miss That Teenage Feeling, *Diagram*
Christmas Night, *Ninth Letter*

NOTES

"Float, Cleave": Facts, quotes, and feelings of total exasperation related to the history of hot air ballooning can be credited to L. T. C. Rolt's *The Aeronauts: A History of Ballooning, 1783–1903* (New York: Walker, 1966). The well-known poet is Ada Limon, who is absolutely right about a great many things. Richard Holmes described Benjamin Franklin's many ingenious plans for hot air balloons in *Falling Upwards: How We Took to the Air* (New York: Vintage, 2014).

"And now brightness falls from the air . . .": Details on the life of Sophie Blanchard come from L. T. C. Rolt's *The Aeronauts: A History of Ballooning, 1783–1903* (New York: Walker, 1966) and Richard Holmes's *Falling Upwards: How We Took to the Air* (New York: Vintage, 2014).

"The Gazelle": For more on the unlikely use of hot air balloons as weapons, see *Balloons at War: Gasbags, Flying Bombs & Cold War Secrets* by John Christopher (Stroud: Tempus, 2004).

"The Blue Sky, the Gray Woods": Information in this essay comes from Charles Coulston Gillespie's *The Montgolfier Brothers and the Invention of Aviation, 1783–1784 with a word on the importance of ballooning for the science of heat and the art of building railroads* (Princeton, NJ: Princeton University Press, 1983), and Richard Holmes's *Falling Upwards:*

How We Took to the Air (New York: Vintage, 2014). Quotes from "Le Beguelle" come from *The Works of Voltaire: The Lisbon Earthquake and Other Poems,* edited by Tobias Smollett and John Morley (Nabu Press, 2012).

"A Thin Blue Line": This essay, too, owes much to Charles Coulston Gillespie's *The Montgolfier Brothers and the Invention of Aviation, 1783– 1784 with a word on the importance of ballooning for the science of heat and the art of building railroads* (Princeton, NJ: Princeton University Press, 1983), as well as L. T. C. Rolt's *The Aeronauts: A History of Ballooning, 1783–1903* (New York: Walker, 1966).

"Heed Not the Milk Hare": We are assured of the historical accuracy of this account of the selection of Louis XIV's bride by Nancy Mitford in *The Sun King* (New York: Harper & Row, 1968). Other details in this essay are drawn from Dennis Todd's *Imagining Monsters: Miscreations of the Self in Eighteenth-Century England* (Chicago: University of Chicago Press, 1995) and Fiona Haslam's *From Hogarth to Rowlandson: Medicine in Art in Eighteenth-Century Britain* (London: Liverpool University Press, 1996). For more on the enigmatic milk hare, see Bodil Nildin-Wall and Jan Wall's "The Witch as Hare or the Witch's Hare: Popular Legends and Beliefs in Nordic Tradition" in *Folklore* Vol. 104, No. 1/2 (1993), pp. 67–76.

"Introduction to the Symbols of the Revolution": All of the details about hairstyles and portraiture come from Caroline Weber's *Queen of Fashion: What Marie Antoinette Wore to the Revolution* (New York: H. Holt, 2006).

"On Horseback": Information about Marie Antoinette's portraits and fashion choices comes from Caroline Weber's *Queen of Fashion: What Marie Antoinette Wore to the Revolution* (New York: H. Holt, 2006). The letters from Marie's mother the empress can be found in *The Letters of Marie Antoinette, Fersen and Barnave,* translated by Mrs. Winifred Stevens and Mrs. Wilfred Jackson (London: John Lane, 1926). A biographical sketch of Théroigne de Méricourt can be found in Galina Serebriakova's *Nine Women: Drawn from the Epoch of the French Revolution,* translated by H. C. Stevens (Freeport, NY: Books for Libraries Press, 1969).

"Plutarch's *Lives of Virtue and Failing*": Charlotte Corday is another of the women chronicled in Galina Serebriakova's *Nine Women: Drawn from the Epoch of the French Revolution,* translated by H. C. Stevens (Freeport, NY: Books for Libraries Press, 1969). *Harper's Weekly* made reference to her case in their April 29, 1865, special edition, *The Murder of the President.*

"Pantoum for Tilly Matthews": All of the details about Tilly Matthews and his influencing machine come from Mike Jay's *The Air Loom Gang* (London: Bantam Press, 2003). A pantoum is a poetic form that involves a pattern of interlocking repeating lines.

"Hearts in Jars": The life and death of Marie Antoinette's children is discussed at length in *Marie Therese: The Fate of Marie Antoinette's Daughter* by Susan Nagel (Bloomsbury, 2007). Julien Raimond's writings can be found in *Slave Revolution in the Caribbean, 1789–1804: A Brief History with Documents by* Laurent Dubois and John D. Garrigus (Palgrave Macmilan, 2006). Details on Haiti's contributions to the French economy and other aspects of the Haitian Revolution come from Laurent Dubois's *Avengers of the New World* (Belknap, 2005).

"Trinkets": Details on the life of Madame de Pompadour come from Nancy Mitford's *Madme de Pompadour* (London: The Reprint Society, 1955), which is part biography and part gossip column, and David Mynder Smythe's more serious *Madame de Pompadour: Mistress of France* (New York: W. Funk, 1953).

"Why the Dauphin Won't Consummate the Marriage": Caroline Weber repeats some of the more popular theories about the dauphin's impotence in *Queen of Fashion: What Marie Antoinette Wore to the Revolution* (New York: H. Holt, 2006). Thomas Kingston Derry's *A Short History of Technology from Earliest Times to A. D. 1900* (New York, Dover, 1960) is an excellent source for information on eighteenth-century locksmithing, though much of his information (including diagrams) is borrowed from Denis Diderot's *Encyclopedia.*

"The Inner Life of Charles-Henri Sanson": Information in this essay is drawn from *Memoirs of the Sansons, from private notes and documents, 1688–147,* which was edited by Henry Sanson, and *Essays on the early period of the French Revolution (1857),* edited by John Wilson Croker, which contains Charles-Henri Sanson's "Memorandum of Observations on the Execution of Criminals by Beheading."

"A Right Cross": For more on the life of the Chevalier d'Éon, see Gary Kates's *Monsieur d'Éon Is a Woman: A Tale of Political Intrigue and Sexual Masquerade* (Johns Hopkins University Press, 2001). For Chevalier de Saint-Georges, Joseph Bologne, see *Monsieur de Saint-Georges: Virtuoso, Swordsman, Revolutionary* by Alain Guédé, translated by Gilda M. Roberts (Picador, 2003).

"Lost Creek Cave": Much of the quail lore in this essay comes from Peter Tate's *Flights of Fancy: Birds in Myth, Legend, and Superstition* (Delacorte, 2008).

"The Known World": There is so much more to know about the folklore related to snakes. Cora Linn Daniels and C. M. Stevens scratch the surface in *Encyclopedia of Superstitions, Folklore, and the Occult Sciences of the World,* volume 2 (Honolulu: University Press of the Pacific, 1903). Vance Randolph's *Ozark Superstitions* (Oxford: Columbia University Press, 1947) is another source of snake folklore for this essay.

"If I make my bed in Hell, you cannot help it, and I will have to lay on it": An exhibition of Jesse Howard's plywood signs and jeremiads was held at the Contemporary Art Museum (CAM) in St. Louis in spring 2015. Howard's art is included in the permanent collections of the American Folk Art Museum and the American Visionary Arts Museum.

"Beset on All Sides": This essay quotes from William James's *The Varieties of Religious Experience: A Study in Human Nature,* which is a compilation of twenty lectures first delivered in Edinburgh and then published in 1902.

"In a Time of Drought": See the chapter on water witching in *Ozark Superstitions* by Vance Randolph (Oxford: Columbia University Press, 1947).

"Fred Sandback Makes Me Miss That Teenage Feeling": The essay draws on hazy memories of *Fred Sandback* (Forum for Contemporary Art, St. Louis, Missouri, March 22–May 18, 1996), as well as his obituary in *The*

New York Times on June 26, 2003, and more recent exhibitions and gallery talks at the Institute of Contemporary Art in Boston.

"Christmas Night": The passages from Anna Akhmatova's *Requiem* quoted in this poem were translated by Judith Hemschemeyer and can be found in *Selected Poems of Anna Akhmatova* (Zephyr, 2000).

"Without or Without You": Look for the TED Radio Hour, "Shifting Time," June 19, 2015, if you want to listen to the interviews for yourself. The radio conversations were with Laura L. Carstensen, PhD, Founding Director of the Stanford Center on Longevity, and Daniel Todd Gilbert, the Edgar Pierce Professor of Psychology and author of *Stumbling on Happiness*.

THE *JOURNAL* NON/FICTION PRIZE
(formerly The Ohio State University Prize in Short Fiction)

Brief Interviews with the Romantic Past
KATHRYN NUERNBERGER

Landfall: A Ring of Stories
JULIE HENSLEY

Hibernate
ELIZABETH ESLAMI

The Deer in the Mirror
CARY HOLLADAY

How
GEOFF WYSS

Little America
DIANE SIMMONS

The Book of Right and Wrong
MATT DEBENHAM

The Departure Lounge: Stories and a Novella
PAUL EGGERS

True Kin
RIC JAHNA

Owner's Manual
MORGAN MCDERMOTT

Mexico Is Missing: And Other Stories
J. DAVID STEVENS

Ordination
SCOTT A. KAUKONEN

Little Men: Novellas and Stories
GERALD SHAPIRO

The Bones of Garbo
TRUDY LEWIS

The White Tattoo: A Collection of Short Stories
WILLIAM J. COBB

Come Back Irish
WENDY RAWLINGS

Throwing Knives
MOLLY BEST TINSLEY

Dating Miss Universe: Nine Stories
STEVEN POLANSKY

Radiance: Ten Stories
JOHN J. CLAYTON